Revolting Jokes

Sandy Ransford has been hooked on humour ever since her first job in publishing – editing the jokes for a well-known magazine – and she has now written more joke books than she can count. Born in South Yorkshire (which may account for it), she now lives in rural mid-Wales surrounded by sheep, with a horse, a cat, two pygmy goats, two miniature ponies and her husband – all of which keep her laughing.

Gerald Hawksley has illustrated lots of books. He lives in Wiltshire with his wife and daughter, a cat, a dog, and a small but persistent goldfish.

Other books by Macmillan

Alien Jokes
Sandy Ransford

2001: A Joke Odyssey
Sandy Ransford

There's a Fly in My Soup
Sandy Ransford

Holiday Jokes
Sandy Ransford

Revolting Jokes

Sandy Ransford

Illustrated by Gerald Hawksley

MACMILLAN CHILDREN'S BOOKS

First published 2002
by Macmillan Children's Books
a division of Macmillan Publishers Ltd
20 New Wharf Road, London N1 9RR
Basingstoke and Oxford
www.panmacmillan.com

Associated companies throughout the world

ISBN 0 330 39773 7

1 3 5 7 9 8 6 4 2

A CIP catalogue record for this book is available from the British Library.

Printed by Mackays of Chatham plc, Chatham, Kent.

Contents

Family and Fiends

JENNY: Auntie Bet fell down the stairs last week.
PENNY: Cellar?
JENNY: No, we think she can be repaired.

BRUCE: Why did you say your uncle had a bitter end?
BRIAN: He drowned in a barrel of beer.

SON: Dad, the man down the road said you weren't fit to live with pigs.
DAD: And what did you say to him?
SON: Oh, I stood up for you. I said of course you were fit to live with pigs.

Mrs Oogle MacBoogle told the police she recognized the man because his head looked just like her husband's behind.

'Mummy, why can't we have a dustbin like other people?'
'Shut up and keep eating.'

ANDY: I don't think my parents like me very much.
AHMED: Why's that?
ANDY: When I asked them for a pet they bought me a piranha fish.

Johnny came rushing into the house. 'Mum!' he yelled, 'I just knocked over that ladder at the side of the house!'

'You'd better tell your father,' replied his mother. 'He was using it to paint the guttering.'

'Oh, he knows already,' replied Johnny. 'He was at the top of the ladder when I knocked it over.'

YOUNG MOTHER: But Harold, that's not our baby!
YOUNG FATHER: No, but it's a much more expensive pram.

FREDDIE: Why does your mum take you to school?
FERGUS: We're in the same class.

FIRST MAN ON GROUSE MOOR WITH RIFLE: I say, sir, you just shot my wife!
SECOND MAN ON GROUSE MOOR WITH RIFLE: I'm very sorry – here, have a crack at mine.

CORONER: You said your wife died after falling down the stairs. Your previous two wives died in car accidents when their brakes failed. It's all a bit strange, isn't it?
MAN IN DOCK: No, you see my third wife couldn't drive.

An accident happened to my brother Jim
When somebody threw a tomato at him.
Tomatoes are squashy and don't hurt the skin –
But this one was specially packed in a tin.

HETTIE: Do you know anyone who's been on the telly?
HATTIE: My little sister did once, but she can use a potty now.

MAN IN SHOP: I'd like a diamond necklace for my wife, please.
SHOP ASSISTANT: I'm sorry, sir, we don't do exchanges.

'Mum, are the Joneses very poor?'
   'I don't think so. Why do you ask?'
   'Well, they made an awful fuss when their baby swallowed a 10p piece.'

BRENDA: I hear you buried your grandpa last week.
GLENDA: We had to, he was dead.

'My husband and I were happy for 25 years.'
'That's good.'
'Yes, then we met.'

'Why did you divorce your husband?'
'He bit his nails in bed.'
'That doesn't sound too awful.'
'No, but these were 15-cm steel ones – he's a joiner.'

'Does your husband have life insurance?'
'No, fire insurance – he knows where he's going.'

'When I looked up my husband's family tree I found half his family were still living in it.'

Little Jimmy came home with blood on his face and a black eye.
   'Who did this to you?' asked his mother.
   Little Jimmy looked grim. 'I don't know his name, but I'd know him if we met again. I've got half his ear in my pocket.'

'Does your sister still walk in her sleep?'
'Not since we covered the floor in tacks.'

'Mummy, Mummy, I don't want to go to Australia.'
'Shut up and keep swimming.'

MOTHER: Why don't you go and play football with your little brother?
CHARLIE: I get tired of kicking him around.

FATHER: Cecil! You eat like a pig! You know what a pig is, don't you?
CECIL: Yes, Dad, a pig is the son of a hog.

'Doctor, my baby just fell down the drain! What can I do?'
'Buy a book on raising children.'

DAD: Who was that at the door?
SON: Someone collecting for the old folks' home.
DAD: Give him your grandad.

SAMANTHA: Mummy, Carol just broke my doll.
MOTHER: How did she do that?
SAMANTHA: I hit her over the head with it.

MRS WOOLLEY: After we'd been married a few years we heard the patter of tiny feet.
MRS WALLY: Was it a boy or a girl?
MRS WOOLLEY: Neither, it was rats.

Why did the monster buy a
hammer?
To burst his pimples.

SALLY: My uncle died last Sunday.
He had a heart attack when he was
down the garden picking runner beans
for lunch.
**SUSIE: How dreadful! What did your
auntie do?**
SALLY: What could she do? She got some frozen
peas out of the freezer.

What did Lot do with his wife after she'd been
turned into a pillar of salt?
Put her in the cellar.

CLARENCE: That's a fine stuffed tiger.
**CUTHBERT: Yes. My grandfather bagged it in
India when he went there with Lord Lottadosh.**
CLARENCE: What's it stuffed with?
CUTHBERT: Lord Lottadosh.

How do you get a paper baby?
Marry an old bag.

MOTHER: Jeremy! I've asked you before! You
must tell me where you buried your father because
he had the car keys in his pocket!

What's old, pink, wrinkled and belongs to Grandma?
Grandpa.

MAN IN HOSPITAL: Does your wife miss you a lot?
SECOND MAN IN HOSPITAL: No, she's a very good shot. That's why I'm here.

LENA: How do you tell if it's raining?
ZENA: I shut my little brother outside and see if he comes in wet.

On a flight from London to New York a child was so badly behaved he annoyed all the passengers. Finally, one man could stand it no longer. 'Hey, kid,' he called, 'why don't you go and play outside?'

MOTHER: Why were you sent home from school?
PAT: Harry was smoking.
MOTHER: But why were you sent home if he was smoking?
PAT: It was me that set him alight.

MOTHER: Caroline! Come in for your dinner! Are your feet dirty?
CAROLINE: Yes, Mum, but I've got my shoes on.

What kind of monster gets up your nose?
A bogeyman.

On which day of the week do monsters eat you?
Chewsday.

What did the monster say to the grand piano?
'What lovely teeth you've got.'

What do his friends sing on the Abominable
Snowman's birthday?
'Freeze a jolly good fellow.'

What do Abominable Snow-mothers have?
Chill-dren.

Deadly Medicine

WILLIE: Does an apple a day keep the doctor away?
BILLY: It does if your aim is good enough.

'Doctor, Doctor, I'm at death's door!'
'Don't worry, I'll pull you through.'

'Doctor, there's something wrong with my stomach.'
'Keep your coat fastened and no one will notice.'

What do you get if someone hits you on the head with an axe?
A splitting headache.

What do surgeons do with their mistakes?
Bury them.

'What should I take when I feel run down?'
'The number of the car that hit you.'

'Doctor, is it true I haven't long to live?'
**'Well, if I were you I wouldn't
start watching any serials.'**

How did the dentist become
a brain surgeon?
His drill slipped.

What's the best way
to avoid catching
diseases from biting insects?
Stop biting them.

DOCTOR: I'm afraid
you've got rabies.
**PATIENT: Quick, give me a piece of paper and a
pencil!**
DOCTOR: Do you want to make your will?
PATIENT: No, a list of people I want to bite.

'Doctor, I think I've broken my leg. What should
I do?'
'Limp.'

HOSPITAL DOCTOR: I'm afraid we have good
news and bad news, Mr Shorty. The bad news is
that we've had to take off both your feet. The good
news is that the man in the next bed wants to buy
your slippers.

How can you cure dandruff?
Cut off your head.

Apprehensive Bertha Bright
Wore her garters much too tight.
Now she walks about on stumps
And comes downstairs in gruesome bumps.

'Doctor, do the tests show I'm normal?'
'Yes, both your heads are quite all right.'

What kind of bandages do people wear after heart surgery?
Ticker tape.

How can you stop a cold in the head from going to your chest?
Tie a knot in your neck.

Why did Cyril take his nose apart?
He wanted to see what made it run.

SURGEON: How's Mr Tiddles after his heart operation?
NURSE: He's doing well but he seems to have two heartbeats.
SURGEON: Ah, I wondered what had happened to my watch.

JENNY: I'm homesick.
MUM: But this is your home.
JENNY: I know, and I'm sick of it.

There was a young lady of Spain
Who was dreadfully sick on a train.
Not once, but again,
And again and again,
And again and again and again.

TIM: I've just swallowed a bone.
TOM: Are you choking?
TIM: No, I'm serious.

What's a chiropodist's
favourite song?
'There's no business like toe business.'

'Doctor, doctor, I feel like a billiard ball.'
'Go to the back of the queue.'

Did you hear about the plastic surgeon?
He sat by the fire and melted.

NURSE: Doctor, this is the second operating table
you've ruined this week.
SURGEON: I must learn not to cut so deeply.

What's bright red and stupid?
A blood clot.

Where do sick ships go?
To the dock.

Was Richard the Lionheart the first transplant
patient?

'Doctor, can you give me something for wind?'
'How about a kite?'

PATIENT: I'm sorry to call you out so late, Doctor.
DOCTOR: That's all right. I had to come out to see someone in the next street so I might just as well kill two birds with one stone.

PATIENT: Doctor, I'm frightened. This is the first time I've had major surgery.
SURGEON: I know how you feel. It's the first time I've done any.

What do you call a fish that performs operations?
A sturgeon.

DOCTOR: You should have sent for me sooner, Mr Twiddle. Your wife is very ill.
MR TWIDDLE: I thought I'd give her a chance to get better first.

NURSE: How's your broken rib?
PATIENT: I keep getting a stitch in my side.
NURSE: That's good, it shows the bones are knitting.

Knock, knock.
Who's there?
Ivor.
Ivor who?
Ivor boil on my bum.

DENTIST: I told you not to swallow. That was my last pair of forceps.

Old Mr Gurgle had a coughing fit and coughed so hard that his false teeth shot across the room, hit the wall, and broke. 'Oh dear,' he mumbled to his friend Mr Gaggle, 'whatever shall I do? I can't afford a new set of teeth.'

'Don't worry,' said Mr Gaggle, 'I'll have a word with my brother. He'll be able to fix you up.'

The next day Mr Gaggle brought Mr Gurgle a new set of teeth which fitted perfectly. 'That's marvellous!' said Mr Gurgle. 'They feel great! Your brother must be a very good dentist to be able to send me the right teeth without even seeing me.'

'Oh, he's not a dentist,' replied Mr Gaggle. 'He's an undertaker.'

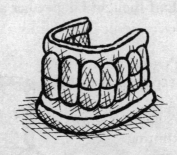

A very mean man was told by his dentist that he'd have to pay £50 to have a tooth out. 'I can't afford that much,' he wailed. 'If I give you £1 could you just loosen it a bit?'

MRS TWIDDLE: I managed to
stop Byron biting his nails.
MRS TWADDLE: How did you
manage to do that?
MRS TWIDDLE: I bought
him some shoes.

What happens when
plumbers die?
They go down the drain.

How can you cure a headache?
Put your head through the window and the pane
will disappear.

How can you tell when someone has a glass eye?
When it comes out in conversation.

'Doctor, I feel half dead.'
'I'll arrange for you to be buried from the waist
down.'

Why did the vampire go to the dentist?
He had fang pangs.

What did one germ say to the other?
'Keep away from me, I think I've got penicillin.'

After an accident a man woke up in hospital with
his face covered in bandages. A doctor said to him,
'You'll be glad to hear that we
managed to save one eye, even
though you're badly hurt.'
   'Oh good,' mumbled the
patient through his
bandages.
   'Yes,' said the doctor.
'And we'll give it to you
as a souvenir when you
go home.'

Mary had a little clock,
She swallowed it one day.
And now she's taking Beecham's pills
To pass the time away.

How can you stop your nose running?
Stick out your foot and trip it up.

Frankly Physical

How can you tell an old person from a young person?
An old person can sing and brush their teeth at the same time.

What should you do when your nose goes on strike?
Picket.

What connects your nose with the Sunday roast?
Dripping.

What's brown and sounds like a bell?
Dung!

What's brown and comes steaming out of Cowes?
The Isle of Wight ferry.

Knock, knock.
Who's there?
Bo.
Bo who?
Bogies up your nose!

What does a man do standing up, a lady do sitting down and a dog do on three legs?
Shakes hands.

JENNY: What do you clean your top teeth with?
BENNY: A toothbrush.
JENNY: And?
BENNY: Toothpaste.
JENNY: And what do you clean your bottom with?
BENNY: The same.
JENNY: Do you? I use paper!

Knock, knock.
Who's there?
Nicholas.
Nicholas who?
Nicholas girls shouldn't climb trees.

Knock, knock.
Who's there?
Saul.
Saul who?
Saul over your shoes, I can smell it from here.

Knock, knock.
Who's there?
Ahab.
Ahab who?
Ahab to go to the loo, open the door!

What do you get if you cross a Persian rug with an elephant?
A large pile on the floor.

Did you hear about the man who was so stupid that when he picked his nose he tore the lining of his hat?

What did the absent-minded skunk say when the wind changed direction?
'Ah, it's all coming back to me now.'

What do you call the little white things in your head that bite?
Teeth.

There was an old man from Darjeeling
Who boarded a bus bound for Ealing.
A sign on the door
Said, 'Don't spit on the floor,'
So he stood up and spat on the ceiling.

What's the difference between fleas and head lice?
Fleas are more crunchy when you eat them.

What has 12 legs, six ears, one eye and a terrible smell?
Three blind mice and half a dead fish.

MRS MACSPORRAN: Your son's very full of himself, isn't he?
MRS MACSLIPPERS: **Yes, especially when he bites his nails.**

What's a sick joke?
Something you shouldn't bring up in polite conversation.

What would happen if pigs could fly?
We'd need very large umbrellas.

What's yellow and smells of bananas?
Monkey puke.

What are long, horny, black and smell of cheese?
Your toenails.

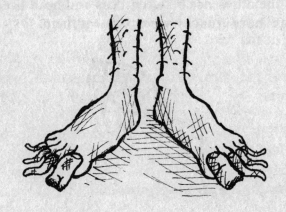

When can't a steam engine sit down?
When it has a tender behind.

What smells awful and shoots soldiers?
A septic tank.

What do you call a man with a lavatory on his head?
John.

What do you call a woman with two lavatories on her head?
Lulu.

Why do traffic lights turn red?
You'd turn red if you had to stop and go in the middle of the road.

Who was the smelliest royal personage in the world?
King Pong.

TEACHER: Now, to help you understand the solar system, let's suppose my hat, here, is Mars. Any questions?
JIMMY: Yes, sir. Is Mars inhabited?

What's a nudist?
A person who wears a one-button suit.

What did one eye say to another?
'Between us is something that smells.'

How do you stop a fish from smelling?
Cut off its nose.

PAUL: Why do you put your hand to your mouth
when you sneeze?
PAULA: To catch my teeth.

Two little girls were paddling at the seaside. 'Coo!'
said one. 'Aren't your feet dirty!'
   'Yes,' replied the other, 'but, you see, we didn't
come last year.'

Mr and Mrs Shufflebottom were on holiday in
Paris. Mr Shufflebottom said to Mrs Shufflebottom,
'Do you realize we've been here a whole week and
we haven't visited the Louvre yet?'
   'Yes,' she replied, 'I expect it's the change in diet.'

What is shampoo?
Imitation poo.

What has a bottom at its top?
A leg.

Which artist specialized in painting nudes?
Bottichilli.

Sam, Sam, the dirty man
Washed his face in a frying-pan.
Combed his hair with a donkey's tail
And scratched his belly with his big toenail.

There once was an old man called Keith
Who mislaid his set of false teeth,
Laid them on a chair,
Forgot they were there,
Sat down, and was bitten beneath.

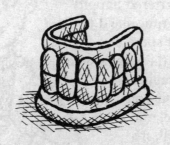

How do we know that Moses wore a wig?
**Because he was sometimes seen with Aaron and
sometimes without.**

MAN ON TRAIN: Do you mind if I smoke?
**SECOND MAN ON TRAIN: Not if you don't
mind if I'm sick.**

Who's there?
Tom Sawyer.
Tom Sawyer who?
Tom Sawyer in the bath.

What do you get if you cross a bear with a pair of very old trainers?
Winnie the Pooh.

Little Louise was given a recorder and a bottle of perfume for her birthday. The following day her parents were entertaining the vicar and his wife to tea. Louise was still feeling very excited about her birthday, and, as she sat opposite the vicar at the tea-table, chattered happily about the lovely time she'd had. 'And did you get some nice presents?' asked the vicar's wife.

'Oh yes,' she replied happily. 'In fact, if you hear a little noise, and smell a little smell, it's me.'

A man was standing by the rail of a ship on a particularly rough crossing. One of the ship's stewards passed by. 'Shall I serve you dinner in your cabin?' he asked.

'No,' groaned the man. 'Just throw it overboard, it'll save me the trouble.'

Knock, knock.
Who's there?
Sonia.
Sonia who?
Sonia shoe, wipe it off before you come in.

Who wrote *A Life on the Ocean Wave*?
Eva Lott.

There was a young lady called Rose
Who had a large wart on her nose.
When she had it removed
Her appearance improved
But her glasses slipped down to her toes.

What's another name for a pair of knickers?
Two policemen.

Who performed the dance of the seven sausage skins
for King Herod?
Salami.

Which famous artist had both an inside and an
outside lavatory?
Toulouse Lautrec.

What's the best place
to have the school
sickroom?
Next to the canteen!

What tree can't you
climb?
A lavatory.

What fruit can you
find in a loo?
A peanut.

Why are non-slip shoes like a spotty schoolboy?
Both have pimples on their bottoms.

Has the bottom fallen out of your world? Eat
prunes, and the world will fall out of your bottom.

Knock, knock.
Who's there?
Blue.
Blue who?
Blue your nose, it's running.

How do you turn ants into undies?
Put a P in front of them.

What's the worst thing you can do to a girl wearing
baggy pants?
Nick 'er elastic.

What do you get if you pull your knickers up to
your armpits?
A chest of drawers.

What did the crew of the sailing boat do when they
became becalmed?
Ate lots of baked beans.

What did one ear say to the other?
'I didn't realize we lived on the same block.'

GINNY: Have you heard what they say about
Donald?
WINNY: No, what's that?
GINNY: That he's got feet worse than death.

Why did Donald's rugby team always win?
**Because their socks smelt so bad no one dared
tackle them.**

What international cricket team plays only half
dressed?
The Vest Indies.

What does a boy do when he wears his pants out?
Wears them in again.

Why were the guards outside Buckingham Palace arrested?
Because they paraded in their bearskins.

Two pigeons were chatting on a rooftop, wondering what to do for a laugh. 'I know,' said one, 'let's go over to that posh car showroom and put a deposit on a new Rolls Royce.'

How do you cope with a gas leak?
Send the person out of the room and open the window.

What's a panther?
A person who makes panths.

What did they do with the farmer who had long, horny toenails?
Used him to plough a field.

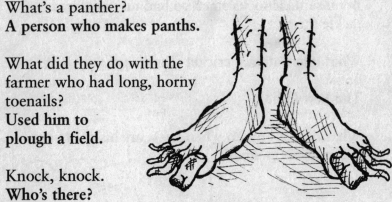

Knock, knock.
Who's there?
Andrew.
Andrew who?
Andrew a rude picture on the blackboard.

KEVIN: What do you call people who live in Europe?
KEITH: European.
KEVIN: No, I'm not, it's just my water pistol that leaks.

Knock, knock.
Who's there?
Adjust.
Adjust who?
Adjust made a mess on the floor.

Knock, knock.
Who's there?
Moppet.
Moppet who?
Moppet up quickly before someone treads in it!

DELIA: There's a wind getting up.
DAHLIA: Here, have an indigestion tablet.

What's the nearest thing to Silver?
The Lone Ranger's bottom.

When is underwear like flowers in the garden?
When it's a pair of pink bloomers.

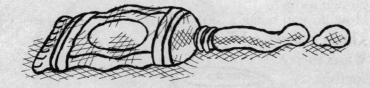

What did the toothpaste say to the toothbrush?
'Squeeze my bottom and I'll meet you outside the tube.'

Knock, knock.
Who's there?
Mustapha.
Mustapha who?
Mustapha wee before I wet my pants.

What did Mr Wobbletum get when he lost five kilos?
The Nobelly Prize.

Knock, knock.
Who's there?
Lou.
Lou who?
Lou's vacant now, you can go in.

What vegetable can you find in a loo?
A leek.

NOTICE IN MEN'S TOILETS:
We aim to keep these toilets clean. Your aim will help.

How do you make a loo roll?
Throw it down a hill.

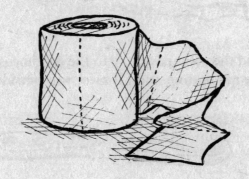

Absolutely Beastly

Did you hear about the dog who lived on garlic?
His bark was worse than his bite!

ANDY: Do you do the pools?
**MANDY: No, it's our new puppy. He's not house-
trained yet.**

What did Tex say when his hound ran under a truck?
'Doggone.'

What happened when the dog ran off with the
skeleton's bones?
He didn't have a leg to stand on.

PADDY: My dog has no tail.
MADDY: How can you tell when he's happy?
PADDY: He stops biting me.

What did the mouse say when his friend broke his
front teeth?
'Hard cheese.'

JERRY: My dog's so lazy.
KERRY: Why do you say that?
JERRY: Yesterday I was watering the garden and he never lifted a leg to help me!

A man walked into a pub with a dog. The landlord looked up and asked, 'What are you doing with that pig?'

The man looked surprised. 'It's not a pig, it's a dog,' he replied.

'I wasn't talking to you,' snarled the landlord, 'I was talking to your dog.'

And did you hear about the stupid dog that lay down to eat a bone?
When it stood up it only had three legs.

Hickory, dickory, dock,
Three mice ran up the clock.
The clock struck one –
The other two got away.

What do you get if you cross a lawnmower with a canary?
Shredded tweet.

What has two heads and five legs?
A horse with a one-legged rider.

GEMMA: You must teach your puppy how to behave. He just bit my ankle.
EMMA: **That's because he's not big enough to bite your neck.**

Every dog has his day but only a dog with a broken tail has a weak end.

A lady with a dog was waiting at a bus stop when up walked a man eating fish and chips. The dog's nose twitched, and he looked longingly at the man's food.

'He likes the smell,' the man said to the lady. 'Do you mind if I throw him a bit?'

'Not at all,' she replied.

So the man picked up the dog and threw him across the road.

Why are pigs unique?
Because after they've been killed they're cured.

LEILA: A shark's just bitten off my foot.
SHEILA: Which one?
LEILA: How should I know? All sharks look the same to me.

NANCY: Our parrot lays square eggs.
CLANCY: Does it talk?
NANCY: Yes, but it can only say one word.
CLANCY: What's that?
NANCY: Ouch!

ALI: There's a big black cat in the garden.
MUM: They're supposed to be lucky.
ALI: This one isn't.
MUM: Why do you say that?
ALI: It just ate next door's dog.

Why can't you hear a pterodactyl go to the toilet?
Because it has a silent p.

DAD: Harold! I hear you got into trouble at the zoo for feeding the penguins! Why was that?
HAROLD: I fed them to the polar bears.

34

What do you get if you cross a flea with a rabbit?
Bugs Bunny.

Two fleas were sitting on Robinson Crusoe's head.
One looked at her watch. 'Time to go,' she said to
the other, 'see you on Friday.'

What goes cluck, cluck, bang!
A chicken in a minefield.

Why did the chicken cross the road?
To prove it had guts.

Why did the elephant cross the road?
To pick up the flattened chicken.

Why did the blind goose cross the road?
To go the the Bird's Eye shop.

How do you stop a skunk from smelling?
Cut off its nose.

What has four legs and flies?
A dead sheep.

MRS TWIDDLE: Have you put the cat out, dear?
MR TWIDDLE: I didn't even know it was on fire.

Why did the lobster blush?
Because the seaweed.

Susie was showing her friend Sally her new pony.
'He's very friendly,' she explained, 'he'll even eat off
your hand.'
    'That's what I'm afraid of,' said Sally nervously.

A man went into a shop, leaving his large Alsatian
dog tied up outside. Just as he was paying the shop
assistant, a lady rushed in and said, 'Is that your
Alsatian tied up outside?'
    'Yes,' said the man. 'Why do you ask?'
    'Well, I'm terribly sorry,' said the lady, 'but I'm
afraid my dog has just killed him.'
    'Killed my Alsatian!' exclaimed the man.

'Whatever kind of dog do you have?'

'A Yorkshire terrier,' replied the lady.

'But how could a tiny Yorkshire terrier kill my great big Alsatian?'

'I'm afraid she got stuck in his throat and choked him to death.'

THEATRICAL AGENT: And what kind of bird impressions do you do, Mr Wisty?
MR WISTY: I eat worms.

DANNY: What's the difference between dog dirt and chocolate?
ANNIE: I don't know.
DANNY: In that case, I'm not sending you out to buy any chocolate!

What's 'amsterjam?
It's like strawberry jam but made from 'amsters.

Two men were laying a fitted carpet in Mrs Kelly's living-room. They had almost finished when one of them reached into his pocket for his packet of peppermints and discovered that they weren't there. 'I must have left them in the van,' he said to his mate.

They carried on fixing the last edge of the carpet and then stood back to admire their work. Right in the centre was a small bulge.

'That must be my peppermints,' said the first man. 'We can't take up the whole carpet again for that, let's just hammer it flat.'

They did so, and then the carpet looked nice and smooth. Mrs Kelly came in to admire it, carrying something in her hand. 'I think one of you must have left these mints in the kitchen,' she said. 'And, by the way, you haven't seen my son's white mouse, have you? He seems to have escaped from his cage.'

What did one tiger say to the other as the Land Rover full of tourists approached?
'Here comes meals on wheels.'

What do you get if you cross a cow with a mule?
Milk that has a kick to it.

How can you tell a skunk from a rabbit?
A skunk uses a cheaper deodorant.

Why did the flea cry?
All his friends had gone to the dogs.

When is a bird in the hand a nuisance?
When you want to pick your nose.

What do you get if you
cross an owl with a skunk?
**A bird that smells and
doesn't give
a hoot.**

What did the baby skunk
want to be when it grew up?
A big stinker.

What should you do if you come across two snails
fighting?
Leave them to slug it out.

As I sat under an apple tree
A birdie sent its love to me.
And as I wiped it from my eye
I said, 'Thank goodness pigs can't fly!'

What has 50 legs and can't walk?
Half a centipede.

What do you get if you cross a young goat with a food mixer?
A crazy mixed-up kid.

TEACHER: Complete this proverb: A bird in the hand . . .
KEVIN: Does it on your wrist.

What do you get if you cross a parrot with a seagull?
A bird that makes a mess on your head and then says sorry.

Knock, knock.
Who's there?
Donna.
Donna who?
Donna sit there, it's where the dog's just been.

A man returned a puppy to its breeder. 'I thought you said this puppy was house-trained,' he complained. 'But it makes a mess everywhere.'

'It is house-trained,' replied the breeder. 'It won't go anywhere else.'

What did one flea say to the other?
'Shall we walk or take a dog?'

What's a polygon?
A dead parrot.

Old Groaners

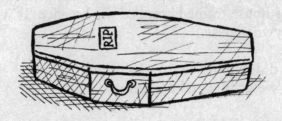

Dr Sawbones lived next door to his most awkward patient, Graham Grumbleton. Several times a week Mr Grumbleton would knock on the doctor's door at all hours of the day or night to ask him to give him some medicine. Once he woke the doctor at 2 a.m. and asked him for something to make him sleep. Another night he woke him at 3 a.m. and asked him for something for indigestion. A third night he asked the doctor for something for his ingrowing toenail.

Dr Sawbones got more and more fed up, and was really very pleased when he heard that the old man had died. 'Ah,' he thought, 'at last I'll get a decent night's sleep.'

But unfortunately for Dr Sawbones, a short while later he was involved in a car accident, and also died. And, as luck would have it, he was buried next to Graham Grumbleton. The following night, the doctor was awakened by a faint knocking on the side of his coffin. 'Doctor,' squeaked a feeble voice, 'can you give me something for worms?'

Hamish and Dougal MacSporran were two not very bright brothers who lived in a cottage high up on a hillside on the outskirts of Aberdeen. They worked in the city, and walked to work each morning and home each night. One cold winter's day, when it was already dark, Hamish was walking home when he began to feel very tired. He was taking a short cut through a graveyard when he spotted a newly-dug grave. 'Hmm,' he thought, 'I could have a quick kip in there.' So he climbed in and instantly fell asleep.

A short while later his brother Dougal was taking the same short cut home. In the dark he tripped over a gravestone, cursed loudly, and sat down to rub his sore toe. The noise woke up Hamish.

'Hello, Dougal, is that yourself?' he called. 'It's very cold here in bed tonight.'

Dougal peered down to look at his brother. 'No wonder you're cold,' he replied, 'you've kicked all the earth off.'

Farmer Giles had a large herd of dairy cows and a few sheep. His neighbour, Farmer Piles, was not the brightest of people. He kept hens, geese – and crows and rooks. Nobody knew why.

One day Farmer Giles met Farmer Piles at the market and they had a chat. Farmer Piles asked Farmer Giles if his cows had produced any good calves recently.

Farmer Giles always felt muddled when he spoke to Farmer Piles. 'Yes,' he replied, 'we've had 20 nice heifers. And how's your farm coming along? Have you bred any good rooks recently?'

Abe and Cabe, two hunters in the Canadian backwoods, were trying to capture some squirrels. They set out armed with a large cage, a gun, and a Rottweiler dog.

Abe said to Cabe, 'I'll climb up a tree and shake the branches. Any squirrels up there will fall down to the ground. The dog will grab them by their tails and keep hold of them, and you can take them off the dog and put them in the cage.'

'Right,' said Cabe to Abe. 'I think I can manage that. But what's the gun for?'

'Ah, well,' replied Abe. 'If I fall out of the tree by mistake, shoot the dog.'

A teacher in a junior school was very upset when she saw a large puddle on the classroom floor. 'Who is responsible for this?' she asked.

The class sat still and didn't say a word. 'Right,' said the teacher. 'Here's a cloth and a bucket of water. We'll all close our eyes while I count to 50 and the person responsible can clean up the puddle. Then we'll never know who did it.'

So the class sat with their eyes closed while the

teacher counted aloud. When they opened their eyes again, they saw a second puddle beside the first and a sign which read: 'The phantom tiddler strikes again!'

Dezzie and Dizzy were out for a walk when they saw two men fishing from a bridge over a river. One man held the other over the bridge's parapet by his ankles while he fished in the water with his bare hands. Every so often he caught a large fish which he threw back to his partner on the bridge.

'That's a good idea,' said Dezzie. 'Shall we have a go?'

'Yes, let's,' said Dizzy.

So they walked on for a while until they came to another bridge. Dizzy volunteered to do the fishing, so Dezzie held him by the ankles. Half an hour passed, but Dizzy caught no fish.

'You're not doing very well,' called down Dezzie.

'No,' began Dizzy, then suddenly he yelled. 'Pull me up quickly, Dezzie, there's a train coming!'

Old Mrs Higginbottom won £10 million on the lottery, but everyone was afraid to tell her about her good fortune in case she had a heart attack. Her doctor called to see her one day and offered to do it for the family. 'Tell me,' he began chattily, 'what would you do if you were to win the lottery?'

'Well, doctor,' she replied after thinking for a while, 'you've always been very kind to me, so I think I'd give half of it to you.' Whereupon the doctor died of shock!

Three cousins, 'Arry, Barry and Carrie, went to see a famous wizard when they were on holiday in central Europe. They were shown all round his castle, including the dungeon. 'If you want a wish granted, you must go into the dungeon alone and say your wish aloud,' said the wizard. 'But take care what you wish for, because you can only have one wish.'

'Arry went down first, and was greeted by the most terrible smell – a mixture of drains and dead rats. Trying hard to ignore it, he said, 'I want to be a famous film star,' and he was transformed into Tom Cruise.

Then Barry went into the dungeon. He, too, managed to ignore the smell, and said, 'I want to be a famous pop star,' and he was transformed into Robbie Williams.

Finally Carrie entered the dungeon. The smell hit her before she could even think about her wish. 'Pooh!' she said – and she was transformed into a bear!

Many years ago a notorious murderer was due to be hanged. On his last morning he was served with a special breakfast and asked if he had any last requests, as was the custom in those days.

He thought for a few moments, and then replied that he would like to sing a song. This seemed a harmless enough request, so the prison governor agreed. So the murderer started to sing: 'There were 999,999,999 green bottles hanging on the wall.'

John and Don both worked at the Kerpow! Gunpowder Works. One day there was a terrible explosion and the members of the company got together to hold an inquiry.

'Now, John, I understand you saw what happened,' said their boss. 'Can you explain what caused the explosion?'

'Well,' began John, 'I'm afraid Don has been getting a bit absent-minded recently. He struck a match and lit his pipe in the factory.'

'He struck a match in the factory?' asked the boss, horrified. 'How long had he worked for us?'

'About 25 years,' replied John.

'Twenty-five years and he struck a match in the factory?' repeated the boss. 'I should have thought that would be the last thing he would do.'

'Yes, it was,' answered John.

A man once bought a very unusual horse which had been trained to obey verbal commands. If his rider said, 'Many,' the horse walked. If he said, 'Few,' it galloped. If the rider said, 'Amen,' the horse stopped.

The man got on quite well with his horse until one day when they were out riding on the downs. A dog ran towards the horse and startled it, sending it galloping wildly towards the cliff edge. In a panic, the man realized he had forgotten the word for 'stop', so as they got ever nearer to the cliff he called out, 'The Lord save us, amen!'

Hearing the word 'amen', the horse obediently stopped. Panting, the rider wiped his brow. 'Phew, that was a close thing . . .' he began.

Greg was working on a building site when he had an accident and his ear was sliced off. All his mates spread out to look for the ear, in the hope that if they found it they could take it to the hospital and it could be sewn back on again. After a few moments one of the men held something up. 'Here it is!' he called. Greg came up to have a look. 'No,' he said. 'That's not my ear. Mine had a pencil behind it.'

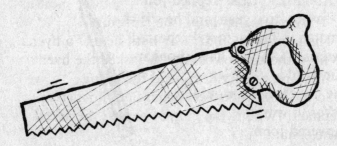

Mrs Tiddles rang her doctor in great agitation. 'What can I do, doctor?' she asked. 'I found my husband asleep with his mouth wide open, and he swallowed a mouse!'

'Go to the fridge and get a lump of cheese,' advised the doctor. 'Tie a piece of string to it and lower it into his mouth. When the mouse grabs the cheese, pull on the string, and you should get the mouse out.'

'Thank you, doctor,' said Mrs Tiddles. 'I'll just nip out and buy a cod's head first.'

'Whatever do you want to do that for?' asked the doctor.

'Oh,' replied Mrs Tiddles. 'I've got to get the cat out first.'

A lion was wandering around when he met a mouse. 'Who is the king of beasts?' he asked the mouse.

'You are, mighty lion,' she replied.

The lion went on his way until he met a hyena. 'Who is the king of beasts?' he asked the hyena.

'You are, mighty lion,' said the hyena.

So the lion walked on again until he met an elephant. 'Who is the king of beasts?' he asked the elephant.

The elephant looked at him, picked him up in his trunk, and hurled him against a tree before dropping him on the ground.

'All right, all right,' said the lion, as he dusted himself down. 'There's no need to get nasty just because you don't know the answer.'

On the Sick List

PATIENT: Doctor, can you cure baldness?
DOCTOR: Certainly. Spread two kilos of pig manure over your head each morning.
PATIENT: Will that make my hair grow?
DOCTOR: No, but no one will come near enough to you to see that you're bald.

PATIENT: Doctor, I'm having trouble breathing.
DOCTOR: I'll soon put a stop to that.

PATIENT: Doctor, I keep thinking I'm a lavatory.
DOCTOR: Hmm, you do look a bit flushed.

ANDY: Are your teeth your own?
MANDY: Whose do you think they are?

Where in Britain can you get new body organs?
Liverpool.

What do you call a woman with only one tooth?
Peg.

NELLIE: Why do you say your brother has Ten Commandments teeth?
SHELLEY: Because they're all broken.

A mother got a bill from the dentist for her young son. It seemed very high, so she rang the doctor and said, 'I thought you charged £20 for a filling, but this bill is for four times that amount.'

'That's right,' answered the receptionist. 'It is £20 but your son screamed so loudly he frightened three other patients away.'

'Jimmy goes to the dentist twice a year.'
'Really?'
'Yes, once for each tooth.'

What did the idiot do with the toothpaste?
Tried to stick a loose tooth in with it.

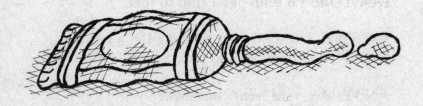

A hospital consultant was doing a ward round. He asked one of his juniors, 'Why is this patient so red in the face?'

'Well, sir,' answered the young doctor, 'it could be because your trousers have just fallen down.'

What happens if you get gastric flu on 24
December?
Christmas 'eave.

MACK: Have you ever had your ears pierced?
MICK: No, but I've had them bored off.

What happens if you eat
uranium?
You get atomic ache.

What do you call a
Spaniard who has just
recovered from an
operation?
Manuel (Man well).

How can you avoid
falling hair?
Jump out of the way.

What's hairy and has a running nose?
A coconut with hay fever.

TEACHER: What do you want to do when you
leave school, Harry?
HARRY: I'd like to follow the medical profession.
TEACHER: You mean you want to be a doctor?
HARRY: No, an undertaker.

MRS WADDLE: I need to lose ten kilos.
MRS WIDDLE: Why not have your head removed?

What happened when the idiot had a brain transplant?
The brain rejected him.

TOMMY: Did you hear that Annie was in hospital?
TIMMY: No, what's wrong with her?
TOMMY: Spotted fever.
TIMMY: Spotted fever? Is that serious?
TOMMY: No, it was spotted in time.

'Doctor, I've got a terrible pain in my lower back.'
'We must get to the bottom of this.'

'Doctor, can you give me something for my liver?'
'How about a rasher of bacon?'

PATIENT: I'm afraid I mistook the medicine you gave me for furniture polish.
DOCTOR: Do you want some more?
PATIENT: No, but you could come round and help me shake the table.

NURSE: This patient doesn't seem to be getting on well with the new drip, doctor.
DOCTOR: No, he was better when Dr Brown attended him.

'Doctor, I've eaten some snooker balls – two red, two black and two pink. What should I do?'
'Eat some greens and you'll soon be all right.'

Why do airlines use the slogan, 'Up and away'?
To remind passengers not to eat too much breakfast.

What is the best cure for air sickness?
Bolting food down.

What happens when a psychiatrist says you're schizophrenic?
He charges you double.

BELLA: You look very red in the face. You must have flu.
ELLA: No, I came on the bus.

A man who consulted his doctor about his poor eyesight was told to eat some carrots. He returned a week later and said that when he'd gone out at night he'd fallen over.
   'Couldn't you see?' asked the doctor.
   'Yes,' replied the patient, 'but I tripped over my ears.'

'Doctor, I feel ill.'
'Just go over to the window and stick out your tongue.'
'Why, so you can see it better?'
'No, because I hate the neighbours.'

If athletes get athletes' foot, what do scientists at the Ministry of Defence get?
Missile toe.

A tourist in the jungle fell ill with a fever and the local witch doctor was called in. He made a dreadful mixture using a frog's tongue, a snake's tail, 12 beetles, three worms and six slugs, all held together with a smear of cow dung. He made the poor man swallow this, and left, saying he would return the next day.

The following morning the witch doctor called to check on the patient. 'Do you feel any better?' he asked.

'No,' groaned the man.

'OK,' said the witch doctor. 'Let's try Plan B.'

'What's Plan B?' asked the patient.

'Two aspirins three times a day,' replied the witch doctor.

'Doctor, I feel like a piano.'
'Hang on a moment while I make some notes.'

Knock, knock.
Who's there?
Juliet.
Juliet who?
Juliet so many cream buns she felt sick.

MOLLY: You're overweight.
POLLY: Nonsense, I'm just 30 cm too short.

Accident Prone

What did the man say after his skiing accident?
'A broken leg isn't all it's cracked up to be.'

Why did the idiot fall out of the window?
Her mother asked her to iron the curtains.

Who exploded at Waterloo?
Napoleon Blownapart.

What do you call a non-swimmer who falls in the river?
Bob.

PASSERBY: Have an accident?
MAN ON STRETCHER: No thanks, I've already had one.

CAROL: My Auntie Olive, who was very rich, fell under a bus last week and died.
CORAL: Oh dear, were you very close?
CAROL: Just close enough to give her a push.

What happened to the burglar who fell in the
cement mixer?
He became a hardened criminal.

DAVE: I'm all red and blistered from sitting in the
sun.
MAVE: Well, I guess you basked for it.

What did the comedian say when someone threw a
turnip at him?
'Would someone like their head back?'

What happened to the man who
struck a match by a gas main?
He rests in pieces.

How did the burglar manage to die
of lead poisoning?
Someone shot him.

What happened to Ray when a
40-tonne lorry
ran over him?
He became Ex-Ray.

FIRST SCHOOLBOY: I
reckon it was better to die
like Joan of Arc than
Charles I.
SECOND SCHOOLBOY: Why do you say that?
FIRST SCHOOLBOY: Because grilled steak is
better than cold chop.

PAT: Will you help me blow up my bike tyres?
MATT: Certainly. Where's the gunpowder?

Why didn't the shark eat the woman who fell
overboard from the ship?
It was a man-eater.

What looks horrible and cuts down trees?
A running sore (saw).

How can a coward prove he has guts?
By lying down on a motorway.

Did you hear about the man who tried to blow up a
bus?
He burnt his lips on the exhaust pipe.

A tourist in Arizona met a Native American who
was lying with his ear pressed to the ground.
    'What are you listening for?' he asked.
    'A stage coach passed here 15 minutes ago,'
replied the Native American.
    'How do you know?' asked the tourist.
    'Because it broke my neck.'

'Auntie Vera was so keen on road safety that she always wore white at night.'
'What happened to her?'
'Last winter she was knocked down by a snow plough.'

Mrs Baggle was talking about her husband. 'When I cut my hand he cried over me.'

'He's very fond of you, is he?' asked her friend Mrs Waggle.

'No,' replied Mrs Baggle. 'He just wanted to put salt in the wound.'

Did you hear about the mean man who on Christmas Eve went out of the house, fired a gun, then came back in and said there would be no presents this year as Father Christmas had just shot himself?

One day a number of small boys, one by one, each confessed to their priest that they had thrown peanuts into the river. The priest was puzzled by their statements, and when yet another lad, this time a rather bedraggled one, came in he said to him, 'I suppose you threw peanuts in the river too?'

'No,' howled the lad. 'I *am* Peanuts!'

What do you do if you split your sides laughing?
Run until you get a stitch in them.

A mountaineer fell down a crevasse and broke both
his arms. His friend threw down a rope, but the
mountaineer couldn't manage to tie it round
himself. 'Grab it in your teeth, then,' called his
friend, 'and I'll pull you up.'
   So the man did this and his friend began to pull
him up. 'Are you all right?' called down the friend.
   'Yeeeees – heeeeelp!' shouted back the
mountaineer.

Another mountaineer got into difficulties when he
was dangling from a rope over the edge of a
precipice. As his friend began to pull him up, the
rope started to fray.
   'What will we do if the rope breaks?' asked the
man fearfully.
   'Don't worry,' called the other man. 'I've got
another.'

BARRISTER IN COURT: And did you see the
defendant bite off Mr Jones's nose?
WITNESS: Not exactly, but I saw him spit it out.

A motorist got a puncture. 'Did you drive over a nail?' asked his wife.

'No, a milk bottle,' replied the man.

'A milk bottle? Couldn't you see it?' asked his wife.

'No, the stupid man had it in his pocket.'

She stood on the bridge at midnight, her lips were
    all a-quiver,
She gave a cough, her leg fell off
And floated down the river.

Mrs Frizzle was busy preparing the dinner when she heard a banging on the stairs. She went into the hall to see her son spreadeagled on the floor.

'Oh dear,' she said. 'Did you miss a step?'

'No,' said the boy ruefully. 'I caught every one.'

A little boy rode round and round the pavements on his bike, leaving behind him a trail of angry pedestrians. Eventually he collided with an old lady. 'Don't you know how to ride that bike?' she yelled.

'Yes,' replied the boy, 'but I don't know how to ring the bell.'

A little girl was walking past a churchyard as it was just going dark when she heard a voice coming from behind a tombstone. 'First I'm going to eat your arms, then I'm going to eat your legs, then your head . . .'

The girl fled, and when she got home told her mother there was a monster in the graveyard eating the bodies. Her mother decided to investigate, and called the police. Together they went back to the graveyard – to find a boy eating jelly babies!

A man waiting at a bus stop took out his eye as the bus drew up, threw it up in the air, caught it and then put it back again.

'Why did you do that?' asked another waiting passenger.

'To see if there was room upstairs, of course,' replied the man.

A policeman patrolling in a city centre one night found a suspicious looking character carrying two heavy suitcases. He pointed to one of them. 'What's in that case?' he asked.

'That's sugar for my tea,' replied the shady character.

'And what's in this case?' persisted the policeman.

'That's sugar for my coffee,' was the reply.

The cop bopped him one with his truncheon.

'Ouch!' said the man. 'What was that for?"

'That's a lump for your cocoa,' replied the policeman.

ANOTHER POLICEMAN: You say he hit you with a shovel?
MAN IN STREET: Yes, and I want him arrested.
POLICEMAN: You don't look as if you've been hit with a shovel.
MAN: You should see the shovel!

Mrs Birdbrain was driving the car while her husband had a nap. He was woken up by her screaming, 'Quick! Take the wheel! There's a tree coming straight for us!'

A man cut his hand badly and went to hospital.
'We'll put a few stitches in that,' said the doctor.

'Right,' said the man. 'And while you're about it, would you sew a button on my shirt?'

Mr Muddlehead's girlfriend and father both had the same birthday. He bought his girlfriend a bottle of perfume, and his father a shotgun, then wrote a note to go with the perfume, saying, 'Use this on yourself and think of me.' Unfortunately he attached it to the wrong present.

A big game hunter was visiting a colleague and he admired a tiger skin rug on the wall. 'He is magnificent,' said the hunter.

'Yes,' replied his host. 'I didn't want to shoot him, but it was him or me.'

'He makes a better rug than you would,' said the hunter.

What a Cheek!

KELLY: How did your brother get that splinter in his finger?
SHELLEY: He scratched his head.

NICK: How long can someone live without a brain?
DICK: I don't know. How old are you?

'My friend said I looked like a werewolf.'
'Shut up and comb your face.'

'She's got a face like a million dollars.'
'Yes, all green and wrinkled.'

SHARON: Do you love me?
DARREN: I'd die for you.
SHARON: You're always saying that but you never do it.

DAVE: How could I ever leave you?
MAVE: By bus, car, train, plane . . .

MICHAEL: If frozen water is iced water, what is frozen ink?
MICHELLE: Iced ink.
MICHAEL: I know you do.

Tracey and Stacey were
discussing a famous beauty.
'Of course,' said Tracey, 'she must be pretty old by now.'
  'Old?' replied Stacey. 'She knew Eve when Eve was Adam's rib.'

SHOPPER: I'd like a dress to match my eyes, please.
ASSISTANT: I'm afraid we don't sell bloodshot dresses.

'She's so good-looking. And she's got long blonde hair all down her back.'
'Pity it's not on her head.'

WILLIE: Who's the blonde with the little wart?
BILLY: Shhh, that's her husband.

CORRIE: Did you miss me while I was away?
LAURIE: Were you away?

TILLY: Did you hear that Mildred had had her face lifted?
MILLY: Who'd want to steal an ugly mug like that?

GWYN: Is that perfume I smell?
LIN: It is, and you do.

DOLLY: What's your new boyfriend like?
POLLY: Oh, he's very polite.
DOLLY: That's nice.
POLLY: Yes. He always takes his shoes off before he puts his feet on the table.

'Is that your face or are you wearing your hair back to front?'

TED: I keep pulling ugly faces.
FRED: Don't worry, people won't notice any difference.

AGGIE: You remind me of a film star.
MAGGIE: Who? Gwyneth Paltrow?
AGGIE: No, Jaws.

ZOE: How dare you tell everyone I'm a silly old fool!
CHLOE: I'm sorry. I didn't know it was a secret.

SIMON: What's that huge, ugly thing on your shoulders?
SUSAN: Ugh, what is it?
SIMON: Your head.

ARCHIMEDES: Eureka!
MRS ARCHIMEDES: You don't smell too good
yourself.

DON: She certainly gave you a dirty look.
RON: Who did?
DON: Mother Nature.

Knock, knock.
Who's there?
Hawaii.
Hawaii who?
I was fine until I met you.

Ken and Len were discussing their
wedding days. 'I got the most
terrible fright,' said Ken.
    'What happened?' asked Len.
    'I married her,' answered
Ken.

'I didn't come here to be insulted!'
'Where do you usually go?'

ROBBIE: What do you think of Walter?
BOBBIE: I'd like to bash his face in, but why
should I improve his looks?

PATTIE: Do you know how to make yogurt?
MATTIE: No, but my mother-in-law does. She
buys a pint of milk and stares at it for a couple of
hours.

BEN: Liza's a slick chick.
KEN: You mean she's like a greasy chicken?

SHEILA: Do you like my new hairstyle?
SHULA: In as much as it covers most of your face, yes.

EILEEN: Why did your sister give her fiancé the push?
AILEEN: He gave her a brass band.
EILEEN: Why did that make her kick him out?
AILEEN: It turned her finger green.

BOB: Dad, there's a man at the door with a nasty look on his face.
DAD: Tell him you've already got one.

'Congratulations! You've just won first prize in our Pull an Ugly Face Contest.'
'Er, but I didn't enter.'

EDWARD: Your sister's spoiled.
EDWINA: No, it's just the perfume she wears.

'The last time I saw a face like yours I threw it a fish.'

HUSBAND: Will you still love me when I'm old and ugly?
WIFE: Of course I do.

'She should have been born in the Dark Ages.'
'Yes, she looks terrible in bright light.'

'I must go now. Don't bother to see me to the door.'
'It's no bother, it's a pleasure.'

ATTENDANT IN THE CHAMBER OF HORRORS: Could you please keep moving on, sir.
VISITOR: Why should I?
ATTENDANT: We're stocktaking and people are getting confused.

MRS BLACK: Why do you want a divorce?
MRS WHITE: My husband smokes in bed.
MRS BLACK: That doesn't sound too dreadful.
MRS WHITE: But it is – he smokes kippers.

MERVYN: What would it take to make you give me a kiss?
MILLICENT: An anaesthetic.

I love you, I love you,
Be my valentine.
And give me your bubble gum –
You're sitting on mine.

A very large man got out of a taxi. As he was paying
the driver, he said, 'You drove here very slowly.'
  'Yes,' agreed the driver. 'But now you've got out
I'll be able to go faster.'

SHARON: Last month I changed my hairstyle, my
make-up, my opinions . . .
DARREN: **Did you change your underwear?**

JO: Your tights are all wrinkled.
MO: **But I'm not wearing any.**

'I never forget a face. But I think in your case I'll
make an exception.'

FRED: You say your brother's an actor. Is he very
good-looking?
TED: **Let's just say he's got a perfect face for radio.**

FIRST COMMITTEE LADY: Oh yes, I throw myself into everything I do.
SECOND COMMITTEE LADY: **Why don't you go and dig a nice big hole?**

LECTURER: My problem is, I don't know what to do with my hands when I'm talking.
COLLEAGUE: **Why not hold them over your mouth?**

GEORGE: I think I've got an inferiority complex.
GORDON: **Nonsense! You *are* inferior.**

ALI: Boys whisper I'm beautiful.
CALLIE: **I bet they don't say it out loud.**

DOREEN: He's a bit overweight, isn't he?
NOREEN: **Let's just say that he has a face that has shipped a thousand lunches.**

A man was driving his car through Surrey and was unsure of the way. So he stopped, wound down his window and called out to a passerby, 'Leatherhead?'
  'Fishface!' came the answer.

'What does your boyfriend do for a living?'
'He's a pig farmer.'
'I thought he had a certain air about him.'

Brenda had been to California and met a famous
film star. 'Is she pretty?' asked Brenda's friend
Glenda.
  'Reading between the lines, yes,' answered
Brenda.

JOE: You have the face of a saint.
JOSH: Thanks, which one?
JOE: Saint Bernard.

MOTHER: What would you say if I sat down at
the table with a face as dirty as yours?
CHARLIE: I'd be too polite to mention it.

LIZZIE: Graham has a heart of gold.
DIZZY: Yes, it matches his teeth.

'He has such an infectious laugh.'
'Well, tell him not to laugh near me.'

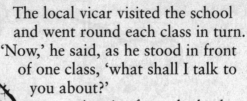

The local vicar visited the school and went round each class in turn. 'Now,' he said, as he stood in front of one class, 'what shall I talk to you about?'

A voice from the back called out, 'About five minutes!'

SAMANTHA: That's my school hat you're wearing.
CAROLINE: No it isn't, yours is the one I dropped in the river.

HENRY: I was at the zoo on Sunday.
HARRY: So was I. It's odd that I didn't see you in any of the cages.

HUSBAND: I'll cook dinner tomorrow. What would you like?
WIFE: Time to take out life insurance.

SINGER: What would you like me to sing next?
MEMBER OF AUDIENCE: Do you know 'Old Man River'?
SINGER: Yes.
MEMBER OF AUDIENCE: Well, go and jump in it.

ARTIST: I've finished painting your portrait. Don't you think it looks like you?
SITTER: Well – it might look better from a distance.
ARTIST: Exactly – just like you.

ERNIE: Did you make my sister cry?
BERNIE: Yes, but I didn't mean to. I paid her a compliment.
ERNIE: What did you say?
BERNIE: I told her she had fewer spots than any girl I'd met recently.

'Looks aren't everything.'
'In your case they aren't anything.'

Three actors were discussing an actress colleague. 'I don't think she has any talent,' said the first.
   'And she's not really that good-looking,' agreed the second.
   'That's right,' said the third. 'I reckon she only got to the top because her dresses didn't.'

'He has a mind of his own.'
'I don't suppose anyone else would want it.'

'She has a sympathetic face.'
'What do you mean?'
'People look at her and feel sympathy.'

DANNY: Have you noticed how Bob drops his Hs?
ANNIE: I've noticed how he drops his vowels – I've got several of his IOUs.

MUM: It was kind of you to let your brother have first go on your new skates.
PAT: I was waiting to see if the ice was thick enough.

JULIE: How old are you?
MUM: **I'm 45 but I don't look it, do I?**
JULIE: No, but you used to.

ROD: Don's wife is like the Mona Lisa.
TODD: **You mean she's beautiful, with an enigmatic smile?**
ROD: No, I mean she's so old she ought to be in a museum.

Mike was listening to his sister singing. 'I wish you'd only sing Christmas carols,' he said.
   'Why's that?' she asked.
   'Then we'd only have to listen to you once a year.'

FRED: Can you help me with my maths homework?
FREDA: **No, it wouldn't be right.**
FRED: I know, but you could try.

HUSBAND: Why are you putting cream on your face?
WIFE: **To make me beautiful.**
HUSBAND: It doesn't work, does it?

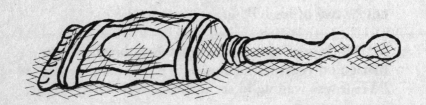

WOMAN AT PARTY: Look at that man over there. He must be the ugliest person I've ever seen.
SECOND WOMAN: He's my husband.
FIRST WOMAN: Oh, I'm so sorry.
SECOND WOMAN: *You're* sorry!

TEACHER: What's your father's name?
SUSIE: The same as mine.
TEACHER: No, his first name.
SUSIE: I don't know.
TEACHER: Well, by what name does your mother call him?
SUSIE: She doesn't call him names, she likes him.

A sailor in uniform was walking through the town when he bumped into a neighbour. 'Hello,' he said, 'I can see you're naval!'

Jess and Tess were talking about an actress on the TV. 'What do you think of her clothes?' asked Jess.
   'I'd say they were specially chosen to bring out the bust in her.'

MICK: I'm a liar, you know.
NICK: I don't believe you.

BERT: Where are you going on Saturday?
BRUCE: To watch United play.
BERT: Do you get very excited when they win?
BRUCE: I don't know, I've only been going for two seasons.

GEMMA: Aren't you going to marry Simon? I thought it was love at first sight.
EMMA: Yes, but the second and third sights put me off.

When Uncle Albert visited, little Linda was allowed to take him a glass of wine. When she'd handed him the glass she stood watching him. 'What do you want?' asked Uncle Albert.

'I'm waiting to see you do your trick,' said Linda.

'What trick?' asked Uncle Albert.

'Well,' said Linda, 'Dad says you drink like a fish.'

'Why does Sean have red hair?'
'He stands on his head a lot.'

What do you get if you cross a nerd with frozen fruit juice?
A wallypop.

A young man was being interviewed by his father-in-law to be. 'So you want to become my son-in-law, do you?' asked the man.

'Not really,' answered the youngster, 'but as I want to marry your daughter I don't have much choice.'

BOSS: Why do you want next Friday off?
YOUNG MAN: I'm getting married.
BOSS: Getting married? What idiot would want to marry someone like you?
YOUNG MAN: Your daughter.

JOLENE: Why did you refuse to marry Darren?
JULIE: **Because he said he'd die if I didn't, and I'm curious.**

She said she wanted to marry a man clever enough to make lots of money, and stupid enough to spend it all on her!

RON: Could you be happy with a boy like me?
CON: **Perhaps, as long as he wasn't too much like you.**

SHARON: My boyfriend says I'm beautiful.
KAREN: **They do say love is blind.**

PETER: Say those three little words that will make me very happy.
ANITA: **Push off home.**

Kate was boasting about her latest conquest. 'He's so good-looking, he's like a Greek statue,' she said.
    'Hmm,' replied her friend Kath. 'And like a Greek statue, he's not all there.'

Jenny was telling Penny how generous her boyfriend was. 'He gave me a mink stole,' she said. Then she added, 'Well, it may not be mink, but it's certainly stole.'

Cyril received a letter from his former girlfriend. 'Dearest Cyril,' it read. 'I am so sorry I called you "Four Eyes" and said I never wanted to see you again. I've had time to think it over, and I'd even marry you if you wanted me to. Do get in touch. All my love, Veronica. P.S. Congratulations on winning the lottery.'

Knock, knock.
Who's there?
Don Giovanni.
Don Giovanni who?
Don Giovanni come and see me any more?

DOREEN: I've just got engaged. Look at this lovely ring.
MAUREEN: Have you got engaged to David Brown?
DOREEN: Yes, but how could you tell, just by looking at the ring?
MAUREEN: I gave it back to him last year.

What did the toe say, when it was asked out on a date?
'I couldn't go out with a heel like you.'

KENNY: If you don't marry me I'll hang myself from a tree in your garden.
PENNY: Please don't, you know how Dad hates people hanging around outside.

SELMA: Is it true you only married Ryan for the money his father left him?
THELMA: Certainly not! I'd have married him whoever had left him the money!

What did the damsel in distress say to the knight? 'Don't just sit there, slay something!'

All in a Day's Work

A secretary went into her boss's office and said, 'I think you're wanted on the phone.'

'What do you mean, you think?' snarled her boss. 'Don't you know?'

'Well,' she replied, 'when I picked up the phone, a voice asked, "Is that you, you silly old berk?"'

A man walking past a building site was hit by a falling brick. 'Oi!' he cried. 'Look out up there! One of your bricks just hit me!'

One of the builders leaned over the scaffolding. 'Then think yourself lucky, mate,' he shouted. 'Look at all the bricks that didn't!'

THEATRICAL AGENT: What kind of an act do you do?
PERFORMER: I'm a contortionist. I bend over backwards and pick up my handkerchief with my teeth.
AGENT: And then?
PERFORMER: Then I bend over again and pick up my teeth.

A young and inexperienced burglar went into a pawnbroker's shop and said, 'Hands up or I shoot!'

The pawnbroker thought rapidly and answered, 'Tell you what, I'll give you £30 for the gun.'

Did you hear about the actor who wanted to play Long John Silver so badly he had his leg cut off? But he didn't get the part. You see, they removed the wrong leg.

FIRST BUSINESSMAN: How's your work coming along?
SECOND BUSINESSMAN: Not bad, but I'm looking for a new cashier.
FIRST BUSINESSMAN: But you only hired one last week!
SECOND BUSINESSMAN: I know, he's the one I'm looking for!

A man worked down the sewers and his friend asked him how he could stand doing such a horrible job. He shrugged his shoulders. 'It may be mucky,' he replied, 'but it's bread and butter to me.'

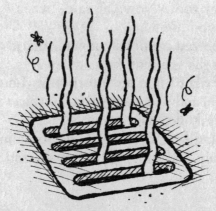

A jeweller was amazed to see a man come hurtling through his window. 'What are you doing?' he called out.

'Sorry,' said the man, 'I forgot to let go of the brick.'

Why did the hangman give up his job?
He didn't like to see people hanging around.

BOSS: Why are you late?
SECRETARY: I fell down some steps and broke my ankle.
BOSS: That's a lame excuse.

BOSS: We start work here at nine sharp.
EMPLOYEE, UNDER HIS BREATH: And we finish at five dull.

Young Andy wanted to join the family business, so his father took him up and sat him on the edge of the factory roof. 'Now,' he said, 'when I say "jump", you jump.'

Andy peered cautiously down. 'But it's nearly 30 metres to the ground!' he said.

'That's right,' said his father. 'But you want to join the business, don't you?'

'I certainly do,' said Andy.

So his father said, 'Jump!' and Andy jumped.

Sitting up and rubbing his bruises and wondering

if he'd broken any bones, he saw his father looking down and laughing at him. 'You've just learned your first, and most important, lesson about business, son,' he said. 'Never trust anybody!'

A woman went to get her hair cut and noticed how dirty the hairdresser's hands were. When she pointed it out, the hairdresser replied, 'No one's been in for a shampoo yet.'

Tilly asked Milly if she still had her job at the florist's.
  'No, I got the sack,' replied Milly.
  'Why?' asked Tilly.
  'I got the cards for the floral tributes mixed up,' answered Milly. 'I sent some flowers to a wedding with a card saying "With deepest sympathy", and some to a funeral with a card that read "I hope you'll be happy in your new home".'

Which singer also worked as a gravedigger?
Bury Many-low.

Some people's work involves writing advertisements and notices – and sometimes they get it horribly wrong! Here's a selection of silly advertisements and printing errors to make you laugh.

Have your children photographed at the convenience of your own home.

Haircut for £4. Children £2.50.

Does your raincoat let in water? Use our waterproofing spray – it will make it really repellent.

Authentic Malaysian food. Eat now – bring back later if not satisfied.

Genuine, strong, hot curries. All our customers are regular.

FOR SALE: Three-bra electric fire.

Order your ring by post. State size or enclose string tied round finger.

Lady seeks two days a week housework – or would divide in two.

Wanted, young assistant to club manager.

FOR SALE: 1920s Rolls Royce hearse. Good condition, original body.

If you shoot yourself and have not tried our cartridges you have missed one of the good things in life.

Save time and cut fingers with our patent multi-blade chopper.

FOR SALE: Pedigree poodle puppies. Sire champion Frizzytop Freddie. Dam well bred.

The way to a man's heart might lie in the art of cooking his liver.

One of the prime requirements of a girl guide is to cook herself.

Climber saved after 12-hour ordeal in bog.

Many passengers hit by cancelled trains.

The Village Society held a swap day on Saturday. Everyone brought something they didn't want. Many ladies brought their husbands.

The bride was upset when one of her bridesmaids trod on her brain and tore it.

A nourishing broth can be made from the remains if someone is unwell in the house.

We regret to announce that Councillor Haversham is recovering from a road accident.

All the drinking water in this café has been personally passed by the manager.

Wet paint – NB this is not an instruction.

The new bride is approximately 75 metres wide from buttress to buttress.

Husbands and children were included in the Women's Institute pot luck supper.

IN A LAUNDERETTE:
Those using automatic washers should remove their clothes when the lights go out.

If the baby does not enjoy cold milk, microwave it.

IN A GERMAN LAVATORY:
Now wash your Hans.

SIGN ON A LAVATORY WALL:
Don't throw your fag ends in the loo
You know it isn't right.
It makes them very soggy and
Impossible to light.

SIGN ON ANOTHER LAVATORY WALL:
In the interests of economy please use both sides of
the toilet paper.

To help the junior football team the sports shop has
kindly donated 12 tracksuit tops and 12 bottoms.

SIGN ON A SEASIDE PIER:
Don't throw people below.

FOR SALE:
FEATHER CUSHIONS. Rock bottom prices.

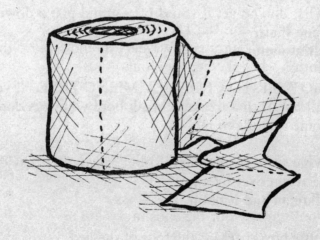

Terrible Fates

BARBER: Were you wearing a red scarf when you came in?
CUSTOMER: No.
BARBER: Oh dear, I must have cut your throat.

What do you get if you drop a grand piano down a mine shaft?
A flat minor.

MOTHER TO CHILD, CLIMBING TREE: If you fall out of that tree and break both your legs don't come running to me!

What were Batman and Robin called after they'd been run over by a bus?
Flatman and Ribbon.

Little boy kneels at the foot of the bed,
Dirty big lump on the top of his head.
Hush, hush, whisper who dares,
Christopher Robin has fallen downstairs.

What goes ho, ho, ho, plop?
Santa Claus laughing his head off.

What happened when the karate expert joined the army?
When he saluted he knocked himself out.

Why did Henry VIII have so many wives?
He liked to chop and change.

What did the prisoner say when he was put on the rack?
'Looks as if I'll be here for a long stretch.'

How can you avoid dying?
Stay in the living room.

How can you sharpen your appetite?
Eat a packet of razor blades.

What do you get if you cross the Atlantic with the *Titanic*?
Halfway.

What's a guillotine?
A pain in the neck.

Young Billy was showing off on his new bike. He whizzed round the drive with his arms folded, yelling out, 'Look, no hands!'

Then he rode round waving his feet in the air. 'Look, no feet!' he shouted.

He carried on like this for a while, until one time he came round, mumbling, 'Look, no teeth!'

A man who had remarried left his son with his new step-mother while he went on a business trip. When he returned he asked his son how he'd got on with her.

'Fine,' replied the lad. 'She took me out on the lake every day in a boat and let me swim back.'

'Did you manage it all right?' asked his father. 'You're not a very good swimmer.'

'The swimming was OK,' said his son. 'The difficult part was getting out of the bag first.'

FIRST MAGICIAN: What happened to that lady you used to saw in half?
SECOND MAGICIAN: She's now living in Manchester and Liverpool.

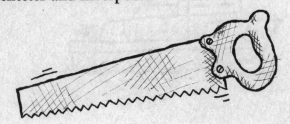

What's the difference between a nail and a boxer?
One is knocked in and the other is knocked out.

What's the most important thing to remember in chemistry?
Don't lick the spoon!

GEORGIE: My uncle disappeared while on a deep-sea diving trip.
GERRY: Really? What happened?
GEORGIE: Something he disagreed with ate him.

DAD: I hate to tell you but your head teacher has fallen down a wishing-well.
JIMMY: It works!

Did you hear about the Irish boy who had a soft spot for his teacher? It was a bog in the middle of Ireland.

Radi was a circus lion,
Radi was a woman hater.
Radi had a lady trainer –
Radiator.

BEN: My mother-in-law is a real treasure.
KEN: **Ever thought of making her buried treasure?**

MINNIE: Have you ever had a hot, passionate, burning kiss?
WINNIE: **I did once. Fred forgot to take his cigarette out of his mouth.**

What time is it when you sit on a drawing-pin?
Spring time.

How do you make a Venetian blind?
Stick your finger in his eye.

How do you make a Swiss roll?
Push him off an alp.

How do you make a Maltese cross?
Pull his ears.

POLICE OFFICER: Did you know your friend fell out of the car back there?
DRIVER: **What a relief! I thought I'd gone deaf!**

PETER: I bumped into old friends yesterday.
ANITA: **You were driving again, were you?**

MUM: Why have you got a
black eye?
DENNIS: I hammered a
thumb in woodwork.
MUM: But that doesn't explain
the black eye.
DENNIS: It wasn't my thumb.

Bessie met a bus,
The bus met Bessie.
The bus was messy,
The mess was Bessie.

TEACHER: What is HNO_3?
SIMON: Er, er, it's on the tip of my tongue . . .
TEACHER: Then you'd better spit it out quickly,
it's nitric acid!

CIRCUS PROPRIETOR: What was the name of
that man who used to put his hand in the lion's
mouth?
LION-TAMER: I can't remember, but they call him
Lefty now.

FIRST EGG: I don't want to go in a pan of boiling
water.
SECOND EGG: It gets worse. When you get out
they bash your head in.

BILL: What would you have if all your fingers were
cut off?
BEN: No more piano lessons!

'Mum, Dad just fell off the roof.'
'I know, I saw him go past the window.'

'When my cousin was born they fired 21 guns.'
'Pity they all missed.'

What do executioners write in December?
Their Christmas chopping lists.

BOB: My grandad says he's got one foot in the grate.
ROB: You mean the grave?
BOB: No, the grate, he wants to be cremated.

KIND AUNT: I was so sorry to hear your head teacher had died. What was the complaint?
LITTLE JIMMY: I don't think there have been any yet.

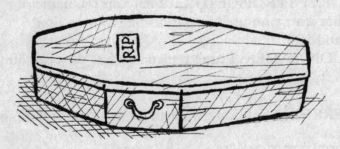

Why did the sword swallower swallow an umbrella?
He wanted to put something by for a rainy day.

Why did the secretary have her fingers cut off?
So she could do shorthand.

DAN: I once swam 800 metres in two seconds.
FRAN: **How on earth did you manage that?**
DAN: I went over a waterfall.

INSURANCE AGENT: This is a very good policy, sir. We pay up to £5,000 for broken arms and legs.
MAN: **Whatever do you do with them all?**

BOB: My wife went on and on about having a new car. She said she wanted a Jaguar.
ROB: **What did you do?**
BOB: I bought her one.
ROB: **And was she happy then?**
BOB: No, it ate her for dinner.

SCIENCE TEACHER: Who can give me the name of a deadly poison?
DONALD: **Parachuting.**
SCIENCE TEACHER: Parachuting? That's not a poison.
DONALD: **One drop and you're dead, though, sir.**

Little Willie, late one night,
Lit a stick of dynamite.
Don't you think he had a cheek?
It's been raining Willie for a week.

A murderer in an American jail was about to be executed by electric chair. The head of the prison asked him if he had any last requests.

'Yes,' replied the condemned man. 'Will you hold my hand?'

MR COOK: Was that cottage pie?
MRS COOK: Yes.
MR COOK: Well, call an ambulance, I think I've just eaten a window.

Why did the farmer laugh when his cow fell over a cliff?
He knew there was no point in crying over spilt milk.

JOHN: What made you become a parachutist?
DON: A plane with three engines on fire.

SEEN SCRIBBLED ON A WALL: Punk is dead.
SEEN SCRIBBLED UNDERNEATH: It certainly smells as if it is.

FREDDIE: I see Dad's got a road map shave again.
TEDDY: What do you mean?
FREDDIE: His face is full of short cuts.

Tommy rushed indoors crying that his friend Timmy had hit him.

'When did he hit you?' asked his mother.

'About half an hour ago,' replied Tommy.

'But I didn't hear you crying then,' said his mother.

'No,' said Tommy. 'I thought you were out.'

ALBERT: Never hit a man when he's down.
ALAN: That's right. He might get up again.

POLICEMAN: How did this accident happen, sir?
DRIVER: Well, constable, you see that sign there that says, 'Stop, look and listen'.
POLICEMAN: Yes.
DRIVER: Well, while I was doing that the train hit my car.

Relatively Speaking

MUM: Why are you crying?
JIMMY: Dad won't play cowboys and Indians
with me.
MUM: Grandad says he will.
JIMMY: He's no good, he's been scalped already.

VICKY: I see your dad's shaved off his beard again.
Why does he keep doing it?
VIOLET: It's Mum, she's been restuffing cushions.

FREDDIE: I saw you kissing my sister last night.
TEDDY: OK, here's £1 to keep your mouth shut.
FREDDIE: Thanks, here's 50p change.
TEDDY: Change? Why?
FREDDIE: I like to be fair, 50p is what I charge the
others.

JENNY: How is your husband's bad back?
GINNY: Not very good. I rubbed it with whisky as
the doctor suggested but he dislocated his neck
trying to lick it off.

SHARON: My husband thought he was a crocodile.
SUSAN: **What did you do about him?**
SHARON: I had him made into a handbag and a pair of shoes.

Why did Mrs Loony keep Mr Loony under the bed?
She thought he was a little potty.

SALLY: Your brother's very economical, isn't he?
WALLY: Well, he saves quite a lot on soap and hot water.

Why was the boy called Squinty?
Because he could see eye to eye with himself.

What is a bigamist?
Someone who makes the same mistake twice.

'Your dad's out of this world.'
'Mum sometimes wishes he were.'

Billy had been out fishing with his little sister. He came back to the house in a bad mood, saying, 'That's the last time I take her with me!'
    'What did she do?' asked his dad. 'Did she frighten off the fish?'
    'No,' answered Billy. 'She ate all my maggots!'

Hans and Gerda were a German brother and sister who were travelling on a train across Bavaria with their mother. Gerda didn't get on with her mother, so when the train slowed at a level crossing, she opened the door and pushed her out, crying, 'Look, Hans, no mum!'

MOTHER: Off you go, all of you, and get in the bath.
VISITOR: Is that how you deal with the rising grime rate in your family?

When two brothers stick together is it because they don't wash very often?

BENNY: How old is your dad?
KENNY: I don't know, but last year there were so many candles on his birthday cake we had to call the fire brigade.

YOUNG MAN: I'd like to have your daughter for my wife.
FATHER: Why, hasn't she got one of her own?

The congregation was filing into a church at a wedding. The usher asked a smartly dressed woman, 'Are you a friend of the bride?'

'Certainly not,' she snapped. 'I'm the groom's mother!'

JOHN: Where's your sister?
DON: She's abroad.
JOHN: I asked where she was, not what she was.

MARY: My granny was a medium.
CARY: Really? Mine was outsize.

MUM: Where are you going?
BASIL: To the cinema.
MUM: What, with dirt all over your face?
BASIL: No, with Bernie next door.

JEAN: What are you going to do when you grow up?
DEAN: Grow a beard so there's less face to wash.

LESTER: Why do you call your little brother
Flannel?
CHESTER: Because he shrinks when we bath him.

The vicar was asking the class what good deeds they had done that week. Lenny put up his hand. 'I did one,' he called out.

'And what was that, Lenny?' asked the vicar.

'Well, there was only one dose of castor oil left and I let my brother have it.'

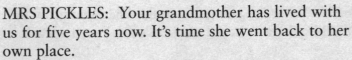

MRS PICKLES: Your grandmother has lived with us for five years now. It's time she went back to her own place.
MR PICKLES: My grandmother? I thought she was yours!

NIGEL: What did you get for Christmas?
NICHOLAS: A drum kit. And it's the best present I've ever had.
NIGEL: Why's that?
NICHOLAS: My dad gives me £5 a week not to play it.

BRIAN: What can I give my sister for her birthday? She's got everything!
BYRON: Penicillin?

SPIKE: What did your dad say when you were sent to prison?
MIKE: 'Hello, son.'

Mr Meanie was on holiday with his wife in a foreign resort and she asked him to buy her a bikini. Grumbling, he went with her to the shop and she chose one. He was horrified when he was told it would cost the equivalent of £65, and even more horrified when the assistant said that price didn't include the tax.

'Tacks?' said Mr Meanie. 'At that price, forget the tacks, she can tie it on!'

MR LOTTADOSH: Why don't you buy your wife a mink outfit?
MR NODOSH: What, a trap and a gun?

BARBER: How do you want your hair cut?
BOY: Like dad's, with a hole on top.

TEACHER: Who can explain the difference between like and love?
JENNY: Well, I like my mum and dad, but I *love* chocolate cake.

TEACHER: If your father borrowed £100 from me and paid me back at £5 a month, at the end of six months how much will he owe me?
ALEC: £100, sir.
TEACHER: You don't know much about arithmetic.
ALEC: And you don't know much about my father!

AGGIE: I can't sleep.
MAGGIE: Why not?

AGGIE: Well, Granny broke her leg and had it put in plaster, and she was told she couldn't climb the stairs.
MAGGIE: How does that stop you from sleeping?
AGGIE: She makes a heck of a racket climbing up the drainpipe.

An aunt who didn't visit very often said to little Billy, 'You've been very nice to me today. I don't believe you want me to go home.'

'No, I don't,' said Billy. 'Dad says he's going to give me a hiding when you've gone!'

The lecturer was droning on and on and his audience was nodding off. 'Can't anything be done to shut him up?' muttered one listener.

'If anything could I'd like to know what it is,' answered his neighbour. 'I'm his wife and I've been trying to shut him up for years!'

The Roundtums were celebrating their wedding anniversary and had a huge, heavy cake. 'My wife made that,' said Mr Roundtum proudly. 'She makes one each year for our anniversary.'

'I suppose,' said his friend, 'you could say they were milestones in your life.'

Anne and Jan were discussing the latest gossip about a TV star. 'Have you seen her latest husband?' asked Anne.

'Yes,' said Jan. 'And I've heard she likes him so much she's decided to keep him another month.'

WIFE: How are you getting on with the lawyers?
WIDOW: We're having so much trouble settling my husband's estate I'm beginning to wish he hadn't died.

A Mixed Bag of Horrors

What's a dirty book?
One that's been dropped in a pigsty.

Why is Westminster Abbey like a fireplace?
Because it holds the ashes of the great (grate).

What is a ringleader?
The first person in the bath.

When does Q come before P?
During the interval at the theatre.

A mother was ticking off her son for fighting. 'You can't have everything in this life,' she told him. 'You must learn to give and take.'
    'But I did,' replied the boy. 'I gave him a cauliflower ear and I took his bar of chocolate.'

What happens when you play table tennis with a bad egg?
First it goes 'ping', then it goes 'pong'.

A Salvation Army girl was doing a collection in the local pub. She waved the plate under the nose of an old man.

'What are you collecting for?' he asked.

'The Lord,' she replied.

'In that case,' said the man, 'you'd better give the money to me. I'll be seeing him before you do.'

What do hangmen read?
Noosepapers.

What do you call a man who's been buried for thousands of years?
Pete (peat).

What's the difference between a lavatory brush and a chocolate biscuit?
You can't dip a lavatory brush in your tea.

How do you spot an idiot at an airport?
He's the one throwing bread to the planes.

How do you spot an idiot in a car wash?
He's the one on the bicycle.

What problem does a man who stands on his own two feet have?
He can't get his trousers on.

JENNY: They say he has a leaning towards pretty girls.
PENNY: Yes, but they push him back.

TEACHER: Give me a sentence containing the word 'gruesome'.
DANNY: Dad didn't shave for a week and grew some whiskers.

MOTHER: You're pretty dirty, Veronica.
VERONICA: I'm even prettier when I'm clean.

Who was Wyatt Burp?
A sheriff with a repeater.

Where in London do people have the worst skin?
'Ackney.

A famous beauty was ticking off her butler. 'You mustn't come into my room without knocking,' she said.
  'Don't worry, Miss,' replied the butler. 'I always look through the keyhole first and if you've no clothes on I don't come in.'

TEACHER: What is a weapon?
JOHNNY: Don't know.
TEACHER: It is something you fight with.
JOHNNY: What, like Cyril?

Why did the ghoul take the dead man for a drive?
Because he was a car-case.

Why did the fat man play the double bass?
Because he couldn't decide which of his chins to put the violin under.

TEACHER: If you're good in this life you will be rewarded with everlasting bliss.
ANDY: And if you're bad do you get everlasting blister?

A vicar was playing golf with a man who kept missing his shots, and each time he missed he exclaimed loudly, 'Damn! I've missed!'

'You shouldn't say that, you know,' protested the vicar. 'The Lord may strike you down.'

Just then there was a vivid flash of lightning from the sky, which struck the vicar and burnt him to a crisp. From out of a cloud came a voice, 'Damn! I've missed!'

BOSS: I'm the boss and you're nothing. What are you?
EMPLOYEE: Nothing.
BOSS: And what am I?
EMPLOYEE: Boss over nothing.
BOSS: Rubbish. You're next to an idiot.
EMPLOYEE: OK, I'll move.

A tourist in a sleepy English village asked a local the age of the oldest inhabitant. 'We ain't got one,' replied the local. 'He died last week.'

MR CRANKY: What did you give your wife for Christmas?
MR CRINKY: A bottle of toilet water. It cost me £25.
MR CRANKY: Good heavens! You could have come round to our house and had water out of the toilet for free.

RADIO ANNOUNCER: The police are looking for a man with one eye called Nelson.
INTERVIEWER: What's his other eye called?

TEACHER: Complete this sentence: A friend in need . . .
DENNIS: . . . is a nuisance.

What does a ghost wear in the rain?
Ghouloshes.

What's a young zombie's favourite toy?
A deady bear.

What did they say about the aristocratic monster?
He was born with a silver shovel in his mouth.

What did the zombie ask the undertaker?
'Do you deliver in my area?'

What training do you need to be a rubbish collector?
None, you just pick it up as you go along.

What did one skeleton say to the other?
'If we had any guts we'd get out of here.'

What do you call a stupid skeleton?
Bonehead.

What did the skeleton get in the Bahamas?
A skeletan.

What did the boy vampire say when the girl vampire walked past?
'Hello, gore juice.'

'Doctor, I think I've been bitten by a vampire.'
'Here, drink this glass of water.'
'Will that make me better?'
'No, but we'll be able to see if your neck leaks.'

What do you get if you cross a vampire with a plumber?
A blood bath.

ANNE: My brother's been practising the violin for years.
JAN: Is he any good at it?
ANNE: No. It took him five years before he discovered you're not supposed to blow it.

A boy stood by the escalator in the Underground station, looking intently at its handrail. 'Are you all right?' asked a worried parent passing by.

'Yes, thank you,' he replied. 'I'm just waiting for my chewing-gum to come round again.'

An earnest young fisher named Fisher
Once fished from the edge of a fissure.
A fish, with a grin, pulled the fisherman in –
Now they're fishing the fissure for Fisher.

What do Chinese cannibals eat?
Chap suey.

Where do cannibals go to school?
Eton.

Why did the cannibal join the police force?
So he could grill his suspects.

Where did the cannibal lady keep her hands?
In a hand bag.

FREDDIE: Did you hear the joke about the cesspit?
TEDDY: No.
FREDDIE: It takes a while to sink in.

Why did Dr Frankenstein go to evening classes?
To do a course on body-building.

Slug Sandwiches

What's worse than finding a slug in your salad
sandwich?
Finding half a slug!

Why do millipedes taste like chewing-gum?
They're wrigglies.

Which town sells meat that makes you ill?
Oldham.

How can you stop fish going bad on Monday?
Eat it on Sunday.

What's a sadist's favourite soup?
Scream of chicken.

Why did the dumbo eat bits of metal all day?
It was his staple diet.

What's yellow, brown and hairy?
Cheese on toast dropped on the carpet.

What do you get if you cross a birthday cake with a tin of baked beans?
A cake that blows out its own candles.

Little Miss Muffet sat on a tuffet
Eating her Irish stew.
Along came a spider and sat down beside her –
And so she ate him up too.

WAITER: Did you like the tongue salad?
DINER: It spoke for itself.

'Waiter! There's a hand in my soup!'
'That's not your soup, sir, that's a finger bowl.'

DINER: What's the difference between the white plate special and the brown plate special?
WAITER: The white plate special costs £2 more.
DINER: But is the food any different?
WAITER: Not usually, it's just that we wash the plate.

WAITER: I have fried liver, steamed tongue and frogs' legs.
DINER: Don't tell me your troubles, just get me the menu.

MRS TRIMBLE: I always shop at Ben the Baker's. They have such lovely warm loaves.
MRS TREMBLE: That's because their cat sits on them all day.

'Waiter! There's a worm on my plate!'
'That's your sausage, sir.'

'Waiter! There's a fly in my soup!'
'That's not a fly, sir, it's the chef. The last customer was a witch doctor.'

'Waiter! There's a fly in my soup!'
'Don't worry, the spider on the roll will catch it.'

Why did Frankenstein's monster get indigestion?
He bolted his food.

What's a vampire's favourite lunch?
Baked beings on toast.

FIRST CANNIBAL:
Who was that lady I saw
you with last night?
SECOND CANNIBAL:
That was no lady, that was
tomorrow's dinner.

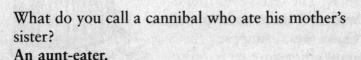

FIRST CANNIBAL: I don't
know what to make of my
husband nowadays.
SECOND CANNIBAL: How
about a curry?

What do you call a cannibal who ate his mother's sister?
An aunt-eater.

What game do cannibals play?
Swallow my leader.

What did the cannibal say after eating the comedian?
'I've got a funny feeling in the pit of my stomach.'

SIGN IN A CANNIBAL'S HUT:
I never met anyone I didn't like.

Why did the cannibal feel queasy after eating the missionary?
You can't keep a good man down.

CANNIBAL MOTHER TO SON: How many times have I told you not to speak with someone in your mouth!

What's a cannibal's favourite meal?
Grilled chaps.

And what's a sea monster's favourite meal?
Fish and ships.

What's a mushroom?
The school dining-hall.

NICK: Where shall we eat?
DICK: The restaurant round the corner seems to be popular.
NICK: Yes, I suppose 10,000 flies can't be wrong.

What did the vegetarian tiger eat?
Swedes.

How do you start a pudding race?
Sago.

How do you start a rude pudding race?
Sago to hell!

SIGN IN A GROCER'S:
Will customers please refrain from sitting on the
bacon slicer as we are getting a little behind with
our orders.

What did the cannibal say when he saw a train
packed with commuters?
'**Oh, good, a chew-chew train.**'

There was a young lady of Riga
Who rode, with a smile, on a tiger.
They returned from the ride
With the lady inside
And the smile on the face of the tiger.

What did the sausage say as it was about to be put
on a skewer?
'**Oh spear me, spear me!**'

What do you get if you cross a pig with a zebra?
Striped bacon.

Why is Camembert
called a two-handed
cheese?
Because you eat it with
one hand and hold your
nose with the other.

Why was the
frankfurter red?
Because it saw the salad dressing.

Why were the tomatoes red?
Because the greengrocer told them rude stories.

A man knocked on the door of a house and asked
for food. The lady who opened the door looked at
him and said, 'Didn't I give you a meat pie last
week?'
  'Yes,' replied the man, 'but I'm better now.'

'Waiter, this food is awful. Bring me the manager.'
'He won't taste any better, sir.'

MRS WIBBLY: I made you a delicious dinner but
the dog ate it.
MR WIBBLY: Don't worry, I expect we can get
another dog.

MR WOBBLY: Is the salad ready, dear?
MRS WOBBLY: How did you know we were
having salad?
MR WOBBLY: I couldn't smell anything burning.

Why was the vampire thin?
He ate necks to nothing.

What do zombies eat with bread and cheese?
Pickled organs.

What's a werewolf's favourite food?
A blood orange.

FIRST CANNIBAL: I've brought a friend home for dinner.
SECOND CANNIBAL: You might have told me. I've spent all day preparing a casserole.

What does 'bacteria' mean?
It's the rear entrance to a cafeteria.

Why are fried onions like a photocopier?
They keep repeating themselves.

What fish tastes good with cream?
A jelly fish.

What do you call a woman who slides around on a piece of hot toast?
Marge.

'Waiter, there's a hair in this honey cake.'
'It must have come off the comb.'

What did one tomato say to the other?
'How did we get into this pickle?'

What's yellow and dangerous?
Shark-infested custard.

FATHER: Come here! I'll teach you to eat your mother's birthday chocolates!
LIONEL: It's all right, I already know how to do that.

What's the difference between school dinners and dog food?
School dinners come on plates; dog food comes in bowls.

KEVIN: This stew's half cold.
MUM: Well, eat the half that's hot.

TERRY: Jim took me to the best restaurant in the West End.
KERRY: **How wonderful! What did you have to eat?**
TERRY: Nothing, he wouldn't take me inside.

WAITER: How is your wood pigeon, sir?
DINER: **Tough.**
WAITER: Would you like a saw and a chisel to eat it with?

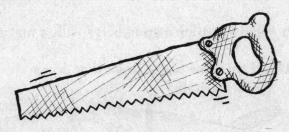

'Waiter, what's this fly doing in my soup?'
'**Looks like the breaststroke, sir.**'

A diner in a restaurant was upset to see a waiter standing scratching his bottom.
   'Excuse me,' he said, 'have you got an itchy bottom?'
   'No sir,' replied the waiter, 'just what's on the menu.'

DINER: These peas are very hard.
WAITER, DIPPING FORK INTO PEAS: **They seem soft enough to me.**
DINER: Yes, they are now, but I've been chewing them for the last half hour.

A very small man went into a café and ordered his food. When he'd eaten his first course he went to get some coffee, then returned to find a very large man sitting in his place.

'Excuse me,' he said timidly, 'but you're sitting in my seat.'

'Prove it,' snarled the large man.

'Certainly,' said the small man. 'You're sitting on my ice cream.'

KATE: Ugh! I just ate a strawberry with a maggot in it!
KEITH: Have some water to wash it down.
KATE: No, let it walk.

DINER: I don't like all the flies in this restaurant.
MANAGER: Tell me which ones you specially dislike and I'll have them thrown out.

'Walls have ears.'
'I think I just found one in my meat pie.'

'Waiter, there's a hair in this pie.'
'Well, you did ask for rabbit pie.'

CLIFF: What's the difference between a sausage roll and a dead rat?
CLARENCE: I don't know.
CLIFF: Then I'll eat the sausage roll and you can have the dead rat.

Even More Beastly

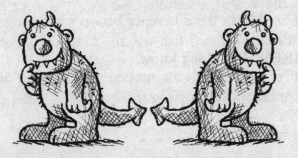

What do you get if you cross a hen with a guitar?
A chicken that makes music while you pluck it.

What do you get if you walk under a cow?
A pat on the head.

DANNY: All the dogs I meet lick my hands.
DAVY: Perhaps if you ate your food with a knife
and fork they wouldn't be so friendly.

Why can't you play a joke on a snake?
You can't pull his leg.

What does a bee sit on?
His beehind.

Why did the bee fly with its back legs crossed?
It was looking for a BP station.

Why don't cows have money?
Farmers milk them dry.

What do you get if you cross a porcupine with a goat?
A kid that's hard to handle.

How did the piranha fish win the football pools?
With eight score jaws.

'You're late,' said one frog to another.
   'I know,' he replied, 'I got stuck in someone's throat.'

Knock, knock.
Who's there?
Jupiter.
Jupiter who?
Jupiter frog in my bed?

What's another name for a mermaid?
A deep-she fish.

What do you get if you cross a hen with a cement mixer?
A brick layer.

Did you hear about the boy who worked at the riding stables?
He complained that his work was piling up.

Why don't centipedes play football?
By the time they've got their boots on it's time to go home.

Why is a rat in the kitchen like a house on fire?
The sooner it's put out the better.

FIRST FLEA: You don't look too well.
SECOND FLEA: No, I'm not feeling up to scratch.

Two goats rummaging on a rubbish tip found a can
of film. So they pulled it out and began to eat it.
'What did you think of it?' asked the first goat.
'Not bad,' replied the second, 'but I think the
book was better.'

What kind of dog has the most ticks?
A watch dog.

What kind of dog did Dracula have?
A bloodhound.

Who herded phantom sheep?
Little Boo Peep.

What did the leopard say when it ate the explorer?
'That hit the spot.'

What do you call a cat's flat?
A scratch pad.

When should you feel sorry for a skunk?
When its spray pump is out of odour.

How do you make mice smell nice?
Use mousewash.

'Why do you call your dog Handyman?'
'He does lots of little jobs round the house.'

I wish I were a cow pat
Sitting in a tree.
And when you came along below
I'd spatter you with me.

MAURICE: What colour are fleas?
DORIS: White.
MAURICE: I thought they were brown.
**DORIS: No, they must be white because Mary had
a little lamb whose fleas were white as snow.**

What did the pig say to the farmer?
'You take me for grunted.'

Two birds were looking at a plane flying across the sky. 'Look how fast it's going,' said the first.

'You'd fly fast if your bum was on fire,' answered the second.

What's red and green and sloppy?
A frog in a liquidizer.

How do you make a snail fast?
Take away its food.

Knock, knock.
Who's there?
Luxembourg.
Luxembourg who?
Luxembourg just did it on your head.

What do you get if you cross a duck with a pig?
Wet and dirty.

What do you call a flea
in an idiot's ear?
A space invader.

A city boy on holiday in
the country heard an owl
hooting. 'What was
that?' he asked.

'That was an owl,'
said his country cousin.

'I know it was an 'owl,' said the city boy. 'But
who's 'owling?'

A man went into a police station carrying a dead parrot, which he said he'd found in his garden. The policeman on duty took down his details, then said, 'OK, if no one's claimed it in six months you can come back and keep it.'

What wears a coat in
winter and pants all
summer?
A dog.

Auntie Elsie was visiting, and
was surprised to see how
friendly the family dog
was. He sat by her
feet, wagged his tail,
and rubbed his head
on her knee.
   'Why is he so friendly?' she asked young Damian.
   'It might be because you've been eating out of his bowl,' he replied.

A woman rang 999 and when her call was answered, asked for a vet.
   'Why do you want a vet?' asked the operator.
   'To open my Rottweiler's jaws,' answered the woman.
   'Then why did you ring 999?' she asked.
   'Because there's a burglar in them.'

Why did the cow jump over the moon?
The milkmaid's hands were cold.

What happened when a farmer emptied a bottle of whisky into his cows' water?
The following day they all had a hangunder.

A motorist ran over a terrier, and went to its owner's door to apologize. 'I'm so sorry,' he said, 'can I replace it?'

'That depends,' said the owner, 'whether you are any good at catching rats.'

Two skunks were being chased by a hunter. As the man got nearer, the first skunk said, 'Whatever shall we do?'

'Let us spray,' replied the second.

JERRY: I washed my parrot in Persil and it died.
PERRY: You shouldn't have washed it in Persil.
JERRY: It wasn't the Persil that killed it, it was the spin dryer.

The animals on the ark were playing football. An ant was just about to score a goal, when an elephant rushed in and squashed him flat.

'You've killed him!' cried the referee.

'I'm sorry,' said the elephant. 'I only meant to trip him up.'

A skunk family had two little skunks they called In and Out. One day little In disappeared. Mother Skunk, Father Skunk and young Out spent hours looking for him, getting more worried all the time. In the end the parents went home to have a cup of tea, but Out said he'd continue searching for a while. Half an hour later he returned home, with a tired In following behind him.

'However did you find him?' asked Father Skunk.

'In-stinct,' replied Out.

What do you call a dream in which you're attacked by a vicious dog?

A bitemare.

Did you hear about the man who boiled a hyena in his cooking pot?

He made himself a laughing stock.

What happens when pigs have dinner?

They have a swill time.

SINGER: Oh dear, I've got a frog in my throat.

MANAGER: Then let him sing, he might have a better voice than you.

Grave Undertaking

What's an undertaker's least favourite motto?
'Never say die.'

What's the underneath of a graveyard called?
The spirit level.

Why is a graveyard noisy?
Because of all the coffin.

What's another name for a coffin?
A snuff box.

Where does an undertaker work?
In a box office.

Why did the undertaker's assistant want to change his job?
He thought it was a dead-end occupation.

JOHN: But why do you want to be buried at sea?
DON: My wife says she wants to walk on my grave.

MR PALEFACE: I think I'm dying.
MRS PALEFACE: Do you have any last requests?
MR PALEFACE: Yes, may I have a piece of that special chocolate cake you made?
MRS PALEFACE: Certainly not, I'm saving it for your funeral.

Old Aunt Jemima enjoyed reading the obituary columns in the newspaper so she could see who had died recently. 'There's just one thing that puzzles me,' she told her son. 'People always seem to die in alphabetical order.'

What do you get if you lean a corpse against a doorbell?
A dead ringer.

SIGN IN A CHURCHYARD:
Will people who have relatives buried here please keep them in good order.

A distinguished explorer and writer was talking to a bright young girl who worked for his publisher. 'I've written a diary of my travels and my life,' he said. 'It is to be published after I'm dead.'

'How interesting,' remarked the girl. 'I can't wait to read it.'

RON: I see old Cyril's died. Did he leave his wife much?
CON: Yes, almost every week.

Why did the cowboy want to die with his boots on?
His socks were full of holes.

One worm was courting another worm in a graveyard. 'Do you really love me?' asked one.
'Oh yes,' replied the other.
'Then come and tell me in dead Ernest,' said the first.

What did the boy maggot say to the girl maggot?
'What's a nice girl like you doing in a joint like this?'

When can't you bury people in a graveyard?
When they're still alive.

Why are you never lonely in a graveyard?
Because there's always somebody there.

CORONER: And what were your husband's last words, Mrs Mouseface?
MRS MOUSEFACE: He said, 'I don't know how that grocer makes a profit selling meat pies at 10p each.'

What were Tarzan's last words?
'Who greased that vine?'

Where did the ghost comedian get his jokes from?
A crypt writer.

What happened when the Swede died?
There was a huge turnip at his funeral.

A funeral procession was making its way slowly along the road. 'Who has died?' a bystander asked a boy who was watching.
   'The man in the coffin,' replied the boy.

What does an undertaker have at 11 a.m. each day?
A coffin break.

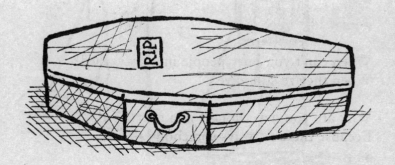

Why did the demon undertaker chop up corpses?
He wanted them to rest in pieces.

How can an undertaker cheer up a corpse?
By telling it every shroud has a silver lining.

How do undertakers speak?
Gravely.

Two zombies went into an undertaker's. The first
said, 'I want to arrange a funeral for a friend who
has just died.'

The undertaker looked at the two of them. 'You
didn't have to bring him with you,' he replied.

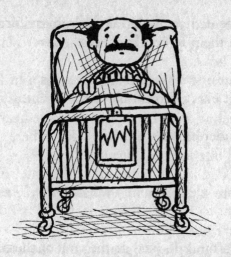

A millionaire was nearly 100 years old and his doctor suggested that maybe he should think about making his will. 'I've already done that,' replied the millionaire. 'I'm going to leave my money to the doctor who saves my life.'

Why should you never trust an undertaker?
Because one day he's bound to let you down.

What do you call the ghost of a sailor?
A sea ghoul.

Why are undertakers often ill?
Because they're surrounded by coffin.

Two boys went out one evening collecting conkers in the local graveyard. They found lots, and when they'd got a huge bagful decided to sit down on a tombstone and share them out. As they were doing so they dropped a couple, which rolled down towards the gate. 'We'll collect those two later,' said one of the boys.

By this time it was getting dark, and a little girl was taking a short cut home through the graveyard. She was feeling a bit nervous, when she heard a voice that stopped her in her tracks. 'There's one for you, here's one for me,' it said.

The girl fled. As she ran out of the gate she bumped into a policeman. 'Whatever's the matter?' he asked.

'There are ghosts in the graveyard,' she stammered, 'and they're sharing out the bodies.'

The policeman accompanied her through the gate. As he did so, he clearly heard the voice, 'There's one for you, here's one for me – and don't forget those two by the gate.'

What's a ghoul's favourite dance?
The last vaults.

A Yorkshire man wanted a headstone put up for his dead wife saying, 'Lord, she was thine.' But when the stonemason had completed it and the man went to check it he found it read, 'Lord, she was thin.'

'This is no good,' he complained angrily. 'You've forgotten the E. You'll have to do it again.'

When the man went to check the headstone again, he found that it read, 'Lord, ee she was thin.'

Little Willie,
Pair of skates.
Hole in ice –
Pearly gates.

Here lies a man who met his fate
Because he put on too much weight.
To overeating he was prone –
Now he's gained his final stone.

Holiday Jokes

Sandy Ransford

Hundreds of hilarious holiday jokes . . .

Where do elephants go on holiday?
Tuskany.

Hotel Guest: Do these stairs take you to the top
floor?
Hotel Manager: No, I'm afraid you'll have to walk.

What did the koala take on holiday?
Just the bear essentials.

What did one rock pool say to the other?
'Show us your mussels.'

Who wrote *Travelling from London to Timbuctoo?*
Miles Apart.

2001

A JOKE ODYSSEY

Sandy Ransford

2001 side-splittingly funny jokes for the millennium ...

Why did the lobster blush?
Because the seaweed.

What do cannibals do at a wedding?
Toast the bride and groom.

What can a whole apple do that half an apple can't do?
Look round.

Why was the mushroom invited to lots of parties?
He was a fungi to be with.

Why is a football stadium cool?
Because there's a fan in every seat.

What do you call a vicar on a motorbike?
Rev.

Alien Jokes

Sandy Ransford

A cosmic collection of hilarious jokes from outer space!

Why was the alien such a good gardener?
Because he had green fingers.

What do you get if you cross an alien with a wizard?
A flying sorcerer.

What's a spaceman's favourite game?
Astronauts and crosses.

Why was the robot so silly?
He had a screw loose.

When's an astronaut's main meal?
Launch time.

A selected list of titles available from Macmillan Children's Books

The prices shown below are correct at the time of going to press. However, Macmillan Publishers reserve the right to show new retail prices on covers which may differ from those previously advertised.

Sandy Ransford

Holiday Jokes	0 330 39771 0	£3.99
There's a Fly in My Soup	0 330 48350 1	£3.50
Alien Jokes	0 330 39219 0	£2.99
2001: A Joke Odyssey	0 330 34988 0	£3.99
Bet You Can't Do This	0 330 39772 9	£3.99
Football Puzzles	0 330 35409 4	£2.99
Christmas Jokes, Puzzles and Poems	0 330 39724 9	£4.99

All Macmillan titles can be ordered at your local bookshop or are available by post from:

Book Service by Post
PO Box 29, Douglas, Isle of Man IM99 1BQ

Credit cards accepted. For details:
Telephone: 01624 675137
Fax: 01624 670923
E-mail: bookshop@enterprise.net

Free postage and packing in the UK.
Overseas customers: add £1 per book (paperback)
and £3 per book (hardback).